# HUNTER HOLMES McGUIRE
## Stonewall Jackson's Doctor

By

John W. Schildt

White Mane Books
Shippensburg, Pennsylvania

Revised Copyright © 2002 by John W. Schildt

ALL RIGHTS RESERVED—No part of this book may be reproduced in any form without permission in writing from the publisher, except by a reviewer who wishes to quote brief passages in connection with a review.

This White Mane Books publication
was printed by
Beidel Printing House, Inc.
63 West Burd Street
Shippensburg, PA 17257-0708 USA

The acid-free paper used in this book meets the guidelines for permanence and durability of the Committee on Production Guidelines for Book Longevity of the Council on Library Resources.

For a complete list of available publications
please write
White Mane Books
Division of White Mane Publishing Company, Inc.
P.O. Box 708
Shippensburg, PA 17257-0708 USA

Library of Congress Cataloging-in-Publication Data

Schildt, John W.
  Hunter Holmes McGuire : Stonewall Jackson's doctor / by John W. Schildt.
    p. cm.
  Includes bibliographical references and index.
  ISBN 1-57249-258-9 (alk. paper)
  1. McGuire, Hunter, 1835-1900. 2. Physicians--Confederate States of America--Biography. 3. United States--History--Civil War, 1861-1865--Medical care. 4. Jackson, Stonewall, 1824-1863--Friends and associates. 5. Confederate States of America. Army of Northern Virginia--Biography. I. Title.

E625.M34 S34 2001
610'.92--dc21
[B]
                                                                          2001057513

PRINTED IN THE UNITED STATES OF AMERICA

With Thanks for the Love and Care
of Dr. Carroll Easterday, and
With Gratitude for the Encouragement of
Dr. Harrison Harbach,
Dr. Richard R. Hoffman, and
Dr. Harold E. Schaden

## Stonewall Jackson's Doctor

a competent physician and surgeon,
a brilliant administrator,
a contributor to the founding of the Red Cross,
a prolific writer on the Civil War, Jackson, and medical subjects,
a gifted teacher and orator,
a pioneer in the medical field,
an advocate of a national department of health,
president of the American Medical Association, and
founder of a hospital.

These and many more were the contributions of Winchester's Dr. Hunter Holmes McGuire.

# Contents

| | | |
|---|---|---:|
| List of Illustrations | | vi |
| Acknowledgments | | vii |
| I | Winchester, Virginia | 1 |
| II | Hunter Holmes McGuire | 3 |
| III | Sparks | 6 |
| IV | Harpers Ferry, Virginia | 8 |
| V | Confederate Medical Service | 11 |
| VI | Battle of First Manassas | 14 |
| VII | Brigade Surgeon | 20 |
| VIII | Back to Winchester | 28 |
| IX | The Valley Campaign | 34 |
| X | The Summer of 1862 | 54 |
| XI | Sharpsburg and Bunker Hill | 58 |
| XII | Fredericksburg and Moss Neck | 68 |
| XIIII | Chancellorsville | 76 |
| XIV | With General Richard S. Ewell | 86 |
| XV | The Year of 1864 | 94 |
| XVI | "Then Cometh the End" | 105 |
| XVII | Richmond, Virginia | 109 |
| XVIII | The Summertime of Life | 117 |
| XIX | At the Confederate Capitol | 125 |
| XX | A Continuing Legacy | 131 |
| Notes | | 134 |
| Bibliography | | 147 |
| Index | | 151 |

# Illustrations

| | |
|---|---:|
| A Surgeon's Kit | 42 |
| A Civil War Ambulance | 42 |
| Samuel Preston Moore | 43 |
| Alexander Swift "Sandie" Pendleton | 43 |
| The Sword Presented to Dr. Hunter McGuire | 44 |
| Staff of General Thomas J. Jackson | 45 |
| Stonewall Jackson's Deathbed, Chandler House | 45 |
| Lieutenant General Thomas J. Jackson | 46 |
| Guiney's Station, Virginia | 47 |
| Jedediah Hotchkiss | 48 |
| A Ransom Note | 49 |
| General Jubal A. Early | 49 |
| Grave of Captain Hugh Holmes McGuire | 50 |
| Mary Stuart | 50 |
| Virginia Hospital | 50 |
| Doctors and Nurses at St. Luke's Home for the Sick | 51 |
| Dr. Hunter McGuire at a Lecture | 51 |
| Grave of Dr. Hunter Holmes McGuire | 52 |
| St. Luke's Hospital | 53 |

# Acknowledgments

A book cannot be written without the assistance of many individuals and libraries. We are grateful for the assistance of Mary McGuire Gilliam of Rockbridge, Virginia; Dr. Hunter Holmes McGuire, Jr., of Richmond, Virginia; and the late Dr. William P. McGuire of Winchester, Virginia, all relatives of Stonewall Jackson's doctor.

The archives of the American Medical Association Library, the Jefferson Medical College, the Medical and Chirurgical Library of the state of Maryland, the Virginia State Library in Richmond, and the Handley Library in Winchester supplied much material for the book. We are appreciative.

Dr. John Lynch, past director of the McGuire Clinic in Richmond, supplied the inspiration needed to carry the manuscript to completion. And thanks to Carole Simcox and JoAnne Knode for typing the manuscript.

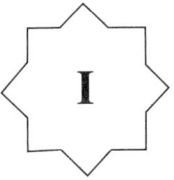

# Winchester, Virginia

Thursday, January 7, 1904, dawned bright and clear. By mid-morning the warm rays of the sun had melted most of the snow that had fallen during the night. Crowds were gathering in Richmond, just north of the capital: families, professional people, and veterans of the War Between the States were coming for the unveiling and dedication of a new monument. Being honored was a doctor, Hunter Holmes McGuire, born in Winchester, Virginia.

Winchester is a small city at the northern end of the Shenandoah Valley in northwestern Virginia.

In 1744, Colonel Joseph Wood named the settlement after his home in Winchester, England. The streets also carried English names, Cork, Amherst, Braddock, Piccadilly, and others. Although founded by the English, most of the first settlers were Germans and Scotch-Irish.[1]

George Washington had an office in Winchester. His task was to survey the vast land holdings of Lord Fairfax. At age 26, Washington was elected to the Virginia House of Burgesses from Frederick County.

Among the early settlers were the McGuires from Fermanagh County, Ireland. Edward McGuire had been involved in an unsuccessful attempt to restore the House of Stuart to power in 1745. Forced to leave Ireland, Edward hoped to join the Austrian army, but was stricken with yellow fever and had to abandon his plans.

In 1747, Edward McGuire landed in Philadelphia, Pennsylvania. He made his way southward to Alexandria, Virginia, and by 1753 settled in Winchester. He soon became very prominent in the community and amassed a small fortune. He built a hotel, and by 1764 owned six thousand acres of land.

McGuire admired culture and education. Among his friends was the Right Reverend John Carroll of Maryland. This distinguished priest became the first American Catholic bishop. His diocese in 1790 included the entire United States.

McGuire donated the money for the construction of the first Catholic Church in the Winchester area. At his death, McGuire was buried under the chancel.

Edward McGuire married Susannah Wheeler of Prince George's County, Maryland. The couple had five children, including a son named Edward, born in Winchester in 1767.[2]

Edward Jr. was an industrious individual. At age 20 he opened his own business in Berryville, Virginia, east of Winchester. Apparently, it was a general store; Edward prospered and soon opened other stores in Winchester, Alexandria, and Norfolk. After managing a thriving business, he suffered financial losses in 1805, and had to start over again—this time as the manager of his father's hotel in Winchester.

Edward Jr. married Elizabeth Holmes,[3] the daughter of Joseph Holmes. To this union seven children were born. Hugh Holmes McGuire was born at the Grove farm five miles south of Winchester on November 6, 1801.

As a lad, Hugh was interested in science and animals. No one was surprised when he decided to be a doctor. At first, he studied under Dr. Robert Barton, the leading doctor in Winchester. Then it was on to the University of Pennsylvania in Philadelphia where he wrote his thesis on tetanus.

Returning to Winchester, the young doctor devoted his time and energy to surgery. He was a pioneer in many fields. Supposedly, he was the first Virginian to perform a cataract operation. Other records indicate that he was the first doctor in America to operate on a patient with a club foot.

Dr. McGuire's fame spread throughout the East Coast. He was invited to teach surgery in medical schools in Philadelphia, New Orleans, and Louisville. However, he preferred contact with patients, and had no desire to leave Winchester. In 1826, McGuire was 25 years old, and in that year he established the Medical School of the Valley of Virginia in his native Winchester.[4] It was the first school of medicine in the Commonwealth.

Three teachers composed the faculty. Dr. McGuire taught anatomy, physiology, and surgery; Dr. John Esteen Cooke taught medicine and obstetrics; and Dr. A. F. Magill, chemistry and materia medica.

The Winchester Medical School flourished for several years. Unfortunately, it was forced to close in 1829 because two-thirds of the faculty accepted other positions. Dr. Cooke[5] went to the University of Transylvania in Kentucky, while Dr. Magill accepted a job at the University of Virginia. Dr. McGuire was also offered several prominent positions, but he turned them down to remain in Winchester and the Shenandoah Valley.

## Hunter Holmes McGuire

Hugh McGuire married Ann Eliza Moss of Fairfax County in 1828. In the next six years, four daughters were born to this union: Gertrude, Margaretta, Anne, and Mary.

The mid-1830s found Dr. and Mrs. Hugh McGuire prospering in their beloved Winchester. Although the school had closed, doctors traveled for miles to consult Dr. McGuire, as he had the gift of being able to quickly diagnose illnesses. He was also one of the best eye surgeons in the East, if not in the nation. The doctor and his wife now lived in a large, elegant brick house on Braddock Street. It was an older home, having been constructed by Lord Fairfax when he came to Winchester.

After four daughters, a son was born on October 11, 1835.[1] The little boy was named Hunter Holmes after Major Andrew Hunter Holmes, an officer who had fallen in the battle of Mackinaw in the War of 1812.

Hunter was to have two brothers: Edward, born in 1837, and Hugh Holmes in 1841. As a boy Hunter enjoyed books and the intellectual stimulation of the home. He joined with other children in spelling bees, taffy pulls, and sledding parties. He grew to be tall, thin, and rather frail looking. From his father, he inherited a love for study and science. Sometimes Hunter rode with Dr. McGuire as he made house calls in Winchester and the surrounding countryside. As a teenager, Hunter was considered a loner, yet he was loved and respected by his peers.

In 1847, Dr. Hugh McGuire reopened his medical school. The name was changed to Winchester Medical College. Dr. McGuire became dean and professor of surgery. State and local funds aided in the purchase of the site. An imposing brick structure, just a few blocks from the McGuire home, was erected. The building included offices, a lecture hall, and surgical rooms. Thirty to forty students enrolled.[2] The quality of training was excellent. No graduate ever failed to pass the test given to those entering military service. Part of this was due to the fact that daily the students had to recite, almost like West Point. There was also individual

*3*

instruction. Young Hunter often went to the medical college with his father. In fact, as a teenager, he took some courses.

Hunter learned the art of the medical profession in Philadelphia. He took some courses at the Pennsylvania Medical College and then transferred to Jefferson Medical College.

In 1857, he was forced to return to Winchester due to an attack of rheumatism. At the age of 22, he was elected professor of anatomy at the Winchester Medical College.[3] One term at home, with his mother's homecooking, helped him gain weight and recover, so he returned to Philadelphia to pursue additional studies.

Hunter McGuire was in Philadelphia at the time of John Brown's raid on Harpers Ferry, October 16, 1859. The raid brought chaos and confusion on college campuses across America. A group of Southern students met to consider their future course of action. Hunter was chosen to be the leader of the group. The young men from south of the Mason-Dixon line frowned upon Brown's raid. They looked upon his men as a group of marauders, respecting neither people nor property. By contrast, the people of the North looked upon Brown as a hero.

During the raid a number of students from the Winchester Medical College went to Harpers Ferry to witness the events. One of the continual problems at the medical school was the lack of cadavers. As the students were leaving Harpers Ferry, they saw the body of one of John Brown's men. They packed the body, the corpse of Owen Brown, in a box and took it back to Winchester for dissection. This event later caused serious trouble for the college.[4]

In December 1859, Brown was hanged in Charles Town. Memorial services were held throughout the North. When Brown's body was carried through the streets of Philadelphia, there was a confrontation between the local residents and the Southern medical students. Blows were exchanged and some of the students were injured. Hunter and one of the faculty members called a meeting of all the Southern students. It was decided that for their own safety, they should leave Philadelphia and return south for the completion of their study.[5]

Hunter telegraphed the Medical College of Virginia in Richmond and asked what terms the students from Philadelphia would receive. The answer was prompt and generous. The students would receive full credit for all previous work completed and could graduate free of charge.

Just prior to Christmas 1859, over three hundred medical students left the school and headed south. When the train reached Richmond, the young men were given a great welcome and marched in a triumphal procession to Capitol Square, where they were greeted by Henry A. Wise, the governor of Virginia. That evening a large patriotic banquet was held in their honor at the Columbian Hotel with over six hundred guests.[6]

Jefferson Medical College was dispirited with the departure of such a large number of students. Some of the officials at the college charged that Hunter McGuire had been bribed or paid to lead the students home. These rumors, although groundless, forced McGuire to leave Virginia. When he arrived in New Orleans he established medical classes at Tulane University. He was very happy in New Orleans, and had the war not come, he might have stayed.

On the eve of the Civil War, young Hunter Holmes McGuire had many assets. He came from a talented and highly respected family, had been exposed to the culture of his day, and had been to schools in the North and South. Likewise, he had experience in medicine. Already a professor, he had a quick mind and a likable personality. A believer in states' rights and the sovereignty of Virginia, his allegiance would be to his native state.

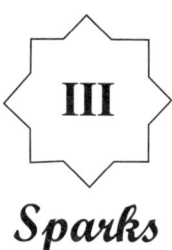

## Sparks

On December 18, 1860, the political leaders of South Carolina convened in Charleston and passed an ordinance of secession. When the last signature was placed on the document, cheers filled the air, bells were rung, and cannon fired. The people of South Carolina had made their choice. Soon Mississippi, Alabama, Georgia, Louisiana, and Texas followed their lead.

Virginia did not follow immediately. In the Shenandoah Valley every county had voted for John Breckinridge, the moderate Democratic candidate. Slavery had been on the decline in the area for many years, and most of the residents "abhorred slavery and stoutly opposed secession."[1] Yet they were Virginians, the Valley belonged to Virginia, and Virginia belonged to the South.

The newspapers in Winchester said that the South was one family...and "if South Carolina secedes and thus inaugurates a final issue with the North, we are necessarily forced to stand in defense of our homes, our interests, and people.[2] However, the residents hoped that war could be averted. Those who studied the situation realized that the location and fertility of the Shenandoah Valley made it a likely target in the event of war. Not only was it an avenue of travel, but it was also a source of food and manpower.[3]

On April 15, 1861, Governor John Letcher of Virginia received a telegram from Washington. From the secretary of war, Simon Cameron, it asked Virginia to provide troops to help quell the rebellion at Fort Sumter. Shots had been fired there a few days earlier. Governor Letcher refused the request, saying, "You have chosen to inaugurate civil war and having done so we will meet you in a spirit as determined as the Administration has exhibited toward the South."[4]

Virginians, including those in the Shenandoah Valley, echoed the feelings of Governor Letcher. They felt they had been insulted by being asked to fight their fellow Southerners. Public opinion and support turned from a wait-and-see attitude to a demand for action. Cornelia Peake McDonald,[5] the wife of Colonel Angus W. McDonald, a wealthy landowner and a relative of Dr. Hunter McGuire, wrote that every person in Winchester "was full of joy; those who a week ago were so violently opposed to secession had completely turned around, and were as ardent as anyone."[6]

The Virginia legislature met in a secret session on April 18–19. The delegates from the cities and counties of the Old Dominion voted 81 to 51 to leave the Union.[7] However, Governor Letcher waited to make the official announcement until another mission could be carried out.

Secret orders had been given to the Virginia militia to seize Harpers Ferry, the northern gateway to the Shenandoah Valley. One of the objectives was the seizure of Federal guns and supplies kept at the arsenal and armory. Federal troops discovered the plot and set fires to destroy the items, thus preventing their capture by the militia. Explosions rocked the town as war had come to the Shenandoah Valley.

Governor Letcher, announcing the vote for secession, called for troops. From all over Virginia, and especially from the Shenandoah Valley, the militia companies answered the call to arms and hastened to Harpers Ferry.

Cornelia McDonald was eating breakfast when the church bells in Winchester began to ring. When she finished, she started work on a dress. Soon, she was overcome with curiosity and went outside to inquire about all the noise. "Virginia has passed the ordinance of secession," she was told. Mrs. McDonald turned away, went back into the house, and folded her pattern. She felt that in the days to come she would have no need for fine dresses.[8]

As national tensions increased, Hunter McGuire left New Orleans and returned to Winchester. He joined the local militia, Company F, Second Virginia Infantry, commanded by Captain William T. Clark. The companies of the Second Virginia were from Charles Town, Shepherdstown, Martinsburg, Winchester, and other nearby places. "The Winchester Rifles" as they were known were in the best position to march and occupy Harpers Ferry.

# Harpers Ferry, Virginia

On the night of April 18, 1861, the sound of explosions filled the air as Union soldiers were blowing up ammunition and other military supplies to prevent them from falling into the hands of the approaching Virginia militia. The men in blue were partially successful, but militia units from nearby Charles Town and Winchester arrived in time to salvage some of the items.[1]

Although it was virtually impossible to defend Harpers Ferry, control of the town was essential. It was the northern gateway to the fertile Shenandoah Valley, a strip of land running nearly three hundred miles north and south between the Allegheny and Blue Ridge Mountains.

Chaos ensued as 4,500 men had gathered at the ferry. A visitor could see all types of weapons and a variety of attire. Many came in their everyday work clothing. Some wore gaudy militia uniforms, and still others were dressed in homespun shirts and coonskin hats.[2]

Thomas J. Jackson, who had taken the cadets of the Virginia Military Institute (VMI) to Richmond, was appointed a colonel of infantry. Robert E. Lee, commander of all the Virginia forces, then ordered Jackson to Harpers Ferry with instructions to take command of the troops.

A graduate of West Point, class of 1846, a veteran of the Mexican War, and a professor for nine years at VMI were Jackson's credentials. Some of his students did not like him because he was so strict. He was also sharp, curt, and to the point. He did not believe in wasting words. To his students, he seemed old-fashioned and eccentric.

Arriving in Harpers Ferry on April 29, his task was to form the undisciplined Virginians into a combat unit and to train and to equip them for the fighting that was ahead.

Companies were reorganized and regiments were created. Camps were laid out and fortifications were constructed. Guards were posted, and strict discipline was enforced. Reveille sounded promptly at 5:00 in the morning, and the rest of the day was devoted to military drill and mastering the art of soldiering.[3] Under Jackson's watchful eye and strict discipline, the men from the Shenandoah Valley were transformed from raw recruits into first-rate soldiers.

In May of 1861, the Confederate government sent Major General Joseph Johnston to Harpers Ferry as Jackson's replacement. Jackson was given command of the First Brigade of the Army of the Shenandoah. The brigade was composed of Virginians of Scotch, Irish, English, German, and Swiss descent. Many were under 21 years of age. The brigade consisted of the Second and Thirty-third Virginia Regiments from the Winchester, Charles Town, and Harrisonburg areas. The Twenty-seventh[4] Regiment came from Lexington and surrounding countryside. The Fourth Regiment of volunteers came from the Tennessee border region. Staunton and Augusta Counties provided the basis for the Fifth Regiment, which was the largest in the brigade. Attached to the First Brigade was the Rockbridge Artillery, commanded by Colonel William Nelson Pendleton,[5] another West Point graduate, and, prior to the war, the rector of the Episcopal Church in Lexington.

Hunter McGuire's brother Hugh had gone to Lexington to attend Washington College. He joined the ranks of the Rockbridge Artillery and was among the thousands gathered at Harpers Ferry. He did not remain with the unit. He was selected to be a private secretary and administrative assistant to Colonel Jackson.

One of the unique units in the First Brigade was Company I of the Fourth Virginia Infantry. They were called the "Liberty Hall Volunteers."[6] Fifty-seven of the 60 members were from Washington College, one-fourth of the unit was studying for the ministry. The Rockbridge Artillery[7] also had 25 men who were theological students.

Many of the volunteers were related. Company C, Fifth Virginia, had 18 members of the same Bell family: six were killed in action and five died of disease during the war. David W. Barton of Winchester gave six sons to the war effort: two were killed, two were wounded.

"Noble state pride and love of home" motivated the men of the Shenandoah Valley to answer the call to arms in the spring of 1861. George Baylor stated, "I felt it my duty to lay down the plow and pruning hook and take up the sword and battle-axe."[8]

Hunter McGuire went to Harpers Ferry as a private soldier in an infantry company. For several weeks he performed routine camp duties, drilled with his comrades, and stood guard.

An administrator in Richmond checking his record saw that he was far too valuable to continue as a front-line soldier. With his medical training and expertise, he was needed as a physician.

The dispatch arrived at Harpers Ferry, and McGuire was ordered to report to Jackson. When the tall, thin, Irishman from Winchester entered the office, Jackson just sat and stared. Finally, the general dismissed McGuire by saying, "You may return to your quarters and wait there until you hear from me."[9]

Days went by and McGuire heard nothing. Then perhaps 10 days later, at a dress parade, the announcement was made, "Dr. Hunter McGuire has been named as the Surgeon of the First Brigade."

Later after becoming better acquainted with the strange man from Lexington, McGuire asked why the delay. Jackson replied, "You looked so young, I sent to Richmond to see if there was some mistake."[10] As brigade surgeon, McGuire assumed the rank of major and the pay of that office. Jackson always referred to his medical director as "Doctor McGuire."

Jackson also had his eye on other young men, seeking those with character and ability for staff positions.

In June of 1861, Alexander Swift "Sandie" Pendleton arrived in Harpers Ferry. He was younger than McGuire, just 20 in the summer of 1861. Jackson had met Pendleton in Lexington where Sandie's dad, the Reverend William Nelson Pendleton, was the pastor of the Episcopal Church. Sandie, considering a ministerial career, was at the University of Virginia when the war broke out. Jackson soon found a job for Sandie on his staff.[11]

Another young man selected for staff duty was Henry Kyd Douglas[12] of Shepherdstown. Like Pendleton, Henry was the son of a minister, and just one day younger than Sandie. Douglas attended Franklin and Marshall College in Lancaster, Pennsylvania. After graduating from college, Douglas went west and practiced law in St. Louis, Missouri. However, when the war broke out, Henry quickly returned home and enlisted in Company B, Second Virginia Infantry.[13]

While Jackson trained the troops at Harpers Ferry, McGuire prepared himself for the battles he knew were to come. He studied about camp diseases and made every effort to stock supplies for his traveling medical wagons. He sought qualified helpers. Like his counterparts in the North, however, the young doctor from Winchester would have to learn from trial and error, experience in camp, and on the field of battle.

By mid-June, Jackson was ready to leave Harpers Ferry. The next month found the First Brigade of the Army of the Shenandoah in what is now the Panhandle of West Virginia. Efforts were made to capture or to destroy railroad stock in Martinsburg. Many nights were spent in bivouac at Camp Stevens, north of Winchester, and McGuire spent some days in the Bunker Hill area.

Jackson's command was well trained by mid-July. Health problems seemed to be at a minimum. Most of the men entered the army in good physical condition. The weather was good, and they benefitted from sleeping under the stars. Disease from fatigue, slim rations, and poor sanitation had not set in.

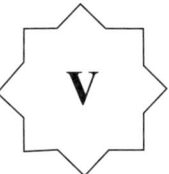

# Confederate Medical Service

In 1861 there were very few hospitals,[1] and hardly any segment of society was prepared for the magnitude of services to be required by the war. Military leaders and physicians were inexperienced in working with large numbers. The U.S. Army numbered less than 20,000 before the wave.

Jefferson Davis appointed Samuel Preston Moore as the surgeon general to the Confederacy. Moore, a native of South Carolina, was nearly 40 years of age. He had served in the army of the United States prior to the war.[2]

Moore had the task of finding doctors, equipment, and supplies for the war effort. The South was very deficient in all three areas. With the physicians mustered into the military, those on the homefront—particularly the young, the women, and the aged—suffered.

Most medical supplies had come from the North. Now these supplies had to be obtained from Europe, and that took time. Often the ships bringing the much needed medical items failed to run the Union blockade of Southern ports.[3]

Many items were smuggled in from the border states and from Washington. Ladies in many areas, either sympathetic or as a humane gesture, made quilts and other items in which they smuggled morphine, quinine, or other medical items in the padding or lining.

McGuire often relied on captured Union medical stores. At least three times in his career he was able to stock his medical chests with Union items. At Winchester in May of 1862, he was overjoyed to gain access to Union supplies. Many items were also captured at Second Manassas, and then supplies and money were obtained in Frederick, Maryland, in 1864.

The men of the South also relied on the resources found in the hills, forests, and fields of their land. There were a lot of home remedies, and the men from the rural areas knew about the power of herbs and teas. At one time there were three pharmacies in the South, using local resources to prepare medicine for the field. One mixture that was used was "old indig" as a substitute for quinine. The bark of the willow, dogwood, and yellow poplar trees was gathered, mashed, and used for treatment.[4]

Surgeon General Moore must have been very efficient. Doctors in the field state that they did not suffer from a lack of the three main drugs: quinine, morphine, and chloroform.[5] Bandages were supplied to the doctors at the front and in the hospitals. Throughout the Confederacy, the women gathered to make bandages. They used old sheets, blouses, and other cotton and linen garments.[6] Material for sutures was smuggled throughout the war. Medical instruments were procured from the stocks of the South, or the doctors brought their own instruments,[7] and some were brought through the blockade.

One of the major items missing from the hands of the army doctors were medical journals or books. Little had been written on the treatment of wounds, and when the war started, there was no time to do much. Therefore, some of the methods had to be learned by on the job training. Later in the war, some copies of *The Confederate States Medical and Surgical Journal* reached doctors in the field. And a Dr. J. J. Chisolm wrote a "Manual of Military Surgery."[8]

Surgeon General Moore organized the Confederate Medical Service in a manner identical to that of the old United States Army in which he had served. There were to be the same regulations, the same ranks, goals, and objectives.

There were only three ranks in the Confederate Medical Service. Surgeon General Moore was at the top as a brigadier general. About one thousand surgeons held the rank and pay of a major of cavalry. Hunter McGuire was in this category. Approximately two thousand assistant surgeons held the rank of a captain of cavalry.

Later in the war, Moore, in an effort to make the medical service more effective, sought legislation creating the office of two assistant surgeons. One would be in charge of the area west of the Mississippi, while the other would act as an administrative assistant to Moore. This bill passed the Confederate Congress but was vetoed by President Davis.

If possible, a surgeon and an assistant surgeon were assigned to each regiment of infantry or cavalry. If manpower permitted, an assistant surgeon was assigned to a unit of battalion size.

The senior physician, the man whose commission bore the oldest date, was normally named brigade surgeon. Although a staff officer, he was not relieved of regimental duties. Naturally, he had all the administrative duties to perform. His men were responsible to him in the chain of command, and he was responsible to his superiors.

With limited means and methods, Surgeon General Moore seems to have done a most commendable job. However, he and his counterparts in the North faced a major problem, for they had little or no experience in handling large numbers of wounded.

Little had been done to improve army medicine since the days of Napoleon. In 1795, Baron Dominique-Jean Larray developed the "flying ambulance."[9] The aim was to remove men as quickly as possible from the fields were they had fallen and get them into a hospital. Jonathan Letterman, the father of the U.S. Army Medical Corps,[10] perfected this plan in the summer of 1862, and put it into operation for the first time at the battle of Antietam. McGuire may have been doing this even earlier. The plan was instrumental in saving men during the Civil War.

Few doctors brought high degrees of speciality to the Civil War. There were very few medical schools prior to the war. Through 1860, Jefferson Medical College in Philadelphia had educated 4,644 physicians, 2,857 from what were to be Confederate states, and 1,787 from the Northern states.[11]

Civil War doctors had basically the same training from the same teachers. The tragic element is that of the more than 11,000 Northern physicians who served during the war, only five hundred had performed surgery. In the Confederacy of three thousand doctors, only 27 had surgical experience.[12] Most of the Civil War doctors performed their first surgery on the battlefield. And even though he was young, McGuire was one of the 27 Southern physicians with surgical experience. The young men who were treated by him were most fortunate.

McGuire was required to send his reports to Richmond to Surgeon General Moore. But the papers he sent, along with those of other Confederate doctors, were destroyed the night of April 2, 1865, when Richmond was swept by fire.

Surgeon General Moore was one of the few efficient cabinet members of the Confederacy. He was strict, stern, and reprimanded many who served under him. Yet, he was quick to encourage and never forgot good work. Naming Moore to be surgeon general was one of the best steps taken by Jefferson Davis.

> Among his achievements were the organization in 1863 of the Association of Army and Navy Surgeons of the Confederate States, 'the oldest American military medical society,' and the sponsoring of important medical publications...He also played a key role in establishing the Confederacy pavilion type hospitals.[13]

# VI

## Battle of First Manassas

As the Army of the Shenandoah assembled and drilled at Harpers Ferry, Union troops were doing the same at Williamsport on the Maryland side of the Potomac to the northwest. Union General Robert Patterson was thought to have around 18,000 troops, while General Joseph Johnston and the Army of the Shenandoah had half that number.

On June 15, 1861, the Confederates burned the bridges at Harpers Ferry and Shepherdstown and started to withdraw to Winchester. Four days later, Colonel Jackson was ordered to Martinsburg to destroy railroad equipment and to watch the enemy.

About four o'clock in the morning on July 2 General Robert Patterson formed his men near Williamsport, crossed the Potomac River, and started advancing toward Martinsburg. He was observed by Colonel James Ewell Brown Stuart and the Confederate cavalry. Word was sent to General Johnston who ordered Jackson and the Virginian troops to the front. Soon Jackson and his newly selected staff were engaged in combat at Falling Waters, just across the Potomac from Williamsport.[1]

Sandie Pendleton's father and the Rockbridge Artillery played a major role in this action. Reverend Pendleton, commanding the artillery, is said to have unlimbered his cannon, nicknamed "Matthew, Mark, Luke, and John," and giving the command, "Aim, fire low, and may God have mercy on their souls."[2]

The action at Falling Waters was little more than a skirmish. The First Brigade, however, did well and gained confidence. The men believed in their cause, in their leader, and in themselves. If the Yankees wanted to move on to Winchester they would receive "a warm welcome." McGuire was happy as there were only a few casualties.

General Johnston observed Jackson in action and saw his skill and leadership ability. As a result, he recommended Jackson for a promotion.

The Army of the Shenandoah moved to the Winchester area. McGuire and many men in the Second Virginia were back home. They were looked upon as heroes because they had turned back the Union advance. Bands played, parades were held, and the soldiers mingled with the pretty girls of Winchester. Each day the ladies of Winchester[3] made bandages for McGuire as well as tents to shelter the wounded and the troops in the field.

Throughout July of 1861, the government in Richmond watched the growing threat of a Union advance against Confederate troops massed near Centreville and Manassas Junction. The Southern forces were commanded by General P. G. T. Beauregard who called for reinforcements.

In answer to that request, about 1:00 A.M. on July 18, General Johnston was awakened by a telegram from Richmond. His army was needed as soon as possible at Manassas.[4]

Acting quickly, Johnston arranged for his sick to be treated in Winchester, while the cavalry screened his departure. Speed and secrecy were of the utmost necessity. The officers and men in the Army of the Shenandoah were angry. No explanation was given for their departure, and they assumed they were running from Union General Patterson. Grudgingly, they moved out of Winchester about noon on the eighteenth.

Leading the way was Jackson's First Brigade. After 90 minutes on the march, Jackson called a halt. General Johnston's order was read to the men: "Our gallant army under General Beauregard is now attacked by overwhelming numbers. The commanding general hopes that his troops will step out like men, and make a forced march to save the country." Cheers swept the line. The First Brigade was ready to go.[5]

The route led to Millwood. About dusk, the troops reached the Shenandoah River. Canteens were filled, and the men started to wade across. On the east side of the river loomed a steep climb, Ashby's Gap. Finally, about two o'clock in the morning of July 19, the weary troops reached the crossroads village of Paris.

In the years that followed, McGuire often talked about the incident at Paris, which led to the poem "The Sleeping Sentinel" by James Ryder Randall. Dr. Robert L. Dabney, a Presbyterian clergyman on Jackson's staff, describes the event:

> Here (at Paris) General Jackson turned his brigade into an enclosure occupied by a beautiful grove, and the wearied men fell prostrate upon the earth without food. In a little time an officer came to Jackson, that reminded him there were no sentries posted around his bivouac, while the men were all wrapped in sleep, and asked if some should be aroused, and a guard set. 'No,' replied Jackson, let the poor fellows sleep; 'I will guard the camp myself....' The remainder of the night he paced around it, or sat upon the fence watching the slumbers of his men.[6]

At the first streaks of dawn, the troops were back on the road. The forced march of 30 miles brought the men to Piedmont Station at the eastern base of the Blue Ridge Mountains. The residents of the village cheered the troops and gave them food. The soldiers boarded cars of the Manassas Gap Railroad for a train ride to the front. Throughout the 19th and most of the 20th, troops were transported to Manassas.

The Confederate line of defense paralleled a little stream known as Bull Run. General Beauregard had stretched his lines along an eight-mile front, trying to cover seven major crossings of the stream. He wanted to protect his rail center at Manassas Junction.

General Irvin McDowell, the Union commander, was forced to take action by the government in Washington. He did not feel that his troops were ready for combat. However, many of his troops were 90-day enlistees, so it was important to fight while he had them available. He had no way of knowing that his opponent had been reinforced by Johnston's forces from the Shenandoah Valley.

Early on Sunday morning, July 21, 1861, Colonel E. P. Alexander, a Confederate officer, detected Union troops moving to the left flank of the Confederate line. Upon receipt of the message, General Nathan G. Evans moved some of his men to oppose the Union advance.

Although slow in executing the attack, the Union infantry was initially successful, and the Confederates were forced back to the hill occupied by the Henry house.

The noise was deafening. Cannon fire, shells bursting, and the constant rattle of musketry made it almost impossible to hear commands. Dr. McGuire gives us his account of First Manassas.

> The Stonewall brigade arrived at Manassas Junction late in the evening of July 20, 1861. We got there after dark, camped alongside the road, and next morning at daylight started to march in the direction of the sound of firing. When Jackson and his brigade arrived very near the field of battle he met Bee's brigade coming back in great disorder. The men had evidently been badly whipped. Jackson carried his men on through these disorganized troops and formed it in line of battle upon the hill. He had been there but a few minutes when a violent attack was made upon the hill by the Federals. Bee, in encouraging his troops to reform and go back to the battlefield, cried out, 'There stands Jackson like a stonewall—rally behind the Virginians.' This is how the name Stonewall originated.[7]

The young doctor from Winchester also gives us the account of Jackson's wound.

> When Jackson made the celebrated charge with his brigade which turned the fortunes of the day, he raised his left hand above his head to encourage the troops, and while in this position the middle finger of the hand was struck just below the articulation between the first and second phalanges. The ball struck the finger a little to one side, broke it, and carried off a small piece of the bone. He remained upon the field wounded as he was till the fight was over, and then wanted to take part in the pursuit.[8]

# Battle of First Manassas

General Johnston ordered him to get the wound treated. Jackson was in great pain, so he stopped at the first-aid station he found. The doctor thought his wound was serious and wanted to amputate the finger. While he went for his instruments, Jackson walked out, mounted his horse, and rode off to find Dr. McGuire.

By this time nearly six hundred men were being treated on the banks of a little stream near the Lewis house. While Jackson was waiting his turn, Jefferson Davis, president of the Confederacy, came galloping up. Davis heard his army had been defeated. His face was pale and his eyes were flashing. "He stood up in his stirrups, glanced over the crowd, and said, 'I am President Davis, all of you who are able, follow me back to the field.'"[9]

McGuire notes what happened next:

> Jackson was a little deaf, and he didn't know who Davis was or what he said until I told him. He stood up at once, took off his cap and saluted the President and said, "We have whipped them, and they ran like dogs. Give me ten thousand men and I will take Washington city tomorrow."[10]

The troops were not available, and it did not seem practical to attack Washington. Now it was time for Jackson to have his finger treated. Dr. McGuire describes the event.

> I was busily engaged with the wounded, but when I saw him coming I left them and asked if he was seriously hurt. 'No,' he answered, 'not half as badly as many here, and I will wait.' And he forthwith sat down on the bank of a little stream near by and positively declined any assistance until 'his turn came.' We compromised, however, and he agreed to let me attend to him after I had finished the case I was dressing when he arrived. I determined to save the finger if possible, and placed a splint along the palmar surface to support the fragments, retained it in position by a strip or two of adhesive plaster, covered the wound with lint, and told him to keep it wet with cold water. He carefully followed this advice. I think he had a kind of fancy for this kind of hydropathic treatment, and I have frequently seen him occupied for several hours pouring cup after cup of water over his hand with that patience and perseverance for which he was so remarkable. Passive motion was instituted about the twentieth day and carefully continued. The motion of the joint improved for several months after the wound had healed, and in the end the deformity was very trifling.[11]

The battle, which started so well for the Union, became a rout, and the First Brigade played a major role in the victory. But in victory and in defeat there are always the dead and wounded. The First Brigade lost 111 dead on the field, and Dr. McGuire had 373 wounded to treat in his various field hospitals, many of them were his friends from the Shenandoah Valley.

Writing home, McGuire said, "The moon was full the night of the battle,...and a more awful sight I never witnessed than that as I went among the dead and wounded of both sides."¹² The battlefield was much different than the classroom or the Winchester office.

Dr. McGuire spent the next three months in the Centreville area. He checked on the progress of the wounded, treated the men who reported on "sick call," and sought to improve the sanitation of the camp area.

Jackson was pleased with the young doctor. Writing in his official report, the general said, "Dr. Hunter McGuire has proved himself to be eminently qualified for his position that of medical director for the brigade."¹³

While at Centreville, McGuire sharpened his skills as brigade surgeon. As the senior doctor, or the physician in charge, the other doctors of the First Brigade reported to him for advice and direction.

As an administrator, he had to check the reports of the other doctors, take corrective measures if possible, and be available for consultation. There were also the weekly, monthly, and quarterly reports to be sent to the surgeon general in Richmond.

After each battle, McGuire compiled the casualty report, dealing with the dead and wounded. He had to be aware of the medical inventory and to requisition the needed medical, surgical, and hospital supplies. It was his responsibility to grant or deny medical furloughs.

As brigade surgeon, McGuire was responsible to his commander, Stonewall Jackson, for the health and welfare of his troops. The brigade surgeon was also the personal physician for the commanding officer and staff. Jackson had his personal health problems. The general's father and sister died when he was but a lad of two years. His mother died when he reached seven. Four years later his grandmother, who had tried to keep the children together, breathed her last. At her death the family was separated, and Thomas went to live with an aunt whom he detested. He ran away several times and went to live with an unmarried uncle who proved to be a help and an inspiration.

Some modern-day psychologists state that these early tragedies gave Jackson an inferiority complex and a very low sense of self-esteem. Those who knew him well thought he was warm and friendly; however, most described him as shy, awkward, and ill at ease.

While growing up Jackson developed a gastric complaint, which bothered him the rest of his life. Probably dyspepsia, or poor digestion, worry and anxiety can make the condition worse. An eye problem that he developed later, along with the dyspepsia, may have been psychosomatic. The symptoms virtually disappeared on the eve of combat, leading doctors to speculate that in battle Jackson had the opportunity to assert himself with anger that he felt over his difficult childhood. His anger could be rent upon the enemy.

Prior to the war, Jackson had gone to various doctors for advice and counseling. He also made frequent trips to health spas, seemingly preoccupied with his gastric problems. This led to strange diets and bizarre behavior. If he sat rigidly at attention or upright, the alimentary canal would be perpendicular, thus aiding digestion. He thought one arm and one leg were too heavy. Hence, he raised them repeatedly to allow the blood to flow back into the body thus making the limbs lighter.

Scholars acknowledge that Jackson was shy, awkward, introverted, and very secretive. He was a very serious person and was rarely known to smile or laugh. This may have stemmed from the unhappiness of his childhood. He was an avid reader of military history, and some maintained that he lived in a world of fantasy. When visiting a historic spot or preparing for battle, he was almost another personality. His clear blue eyes flashed with the light of battle, his nostrils quivered with emotion, his voice barked commands, and then he waved his men forward.

He was a man of great personal discipline. Modern psychologists contend that he needed this to keep his anger and aggression under control, and often this resulted in the psychosomatic gastric and eye problems. Deeply religious, he believed God would take care of him, and he thrived on the dangers and difficulties of warfare. "Always mislead and mystify your enemy."

After First Manassas, Dr. McGuire had his hands full treating those who were sick and those suffering from various diseases. In August 1862, a North Carolina soldier wrote home saying the "these Big Battles is not as bad as the fever." Later a soldier from Ohio wrote that "there is more dies by sickness than gets killed."[14]

McGuire and the First Brigade experienced this reality shortly after the battle of Manassas. Camped near the battlefield, the odor of decaying flesh filled the air. The water supply was contaminated. The soldiers named the bivouac area "Camp Maggot."[15] Cases of typhoid fever began to develop until the campsite was then moved one mile east of Centreville.

# VII

## *Brigade Surgeon*

Throughout the war problems such as this continued to plague McGuire and physicians, on both sides. Sickness and disease took a terrific toll. In the Union army, 360,222 men died during the war, 110,070 in battle-related deaths, and the rest from disease. Although Confederate records are incomplete, the best estimate is that 258,000 died. Of these, 94,000 died in combat, and 164,000 from sickness[1] or causes not associated with battle. Society, the medical profession included, was largely ignorant of the cause of disease. Little was known about bacteriology. Malaria was attributed to the fumes and vapor drifting through the swamps.

Recruits and prospects were not carefully screened at the induction centers. Thus some men entered service with tuberculosis and other infectious diseases. Others enlisted but were in such poor physical condition that they fell victim to the first epidemic to sweep the camp.

Another contributing factor was the diet. The Union forces generally fared much better than their counterparts in the South. Fresh fruits and vegetables were generally nonexistent in the Army of Northern Virginia. After a while, fresh milk became very scarce. Meat was cooked in grease, and often the men had spoiled meat distributed to them. Little was known about vitamins and a balanced diet. The sutlers sold what we might consider the junk food of that day, pies and cakes. The Army of Northern Virginia suffered greatly in the Maryland campaign as the men subsisted on green corn and green apples.[2] A Union doctor examining the Confederate campsites said that evidence of diarrhea could be seen at the latrine areas of every bivouac area.[3]

Shelter and clothing were insufficient to protect the troops from the elements. Soldiers of both armies got soaked and chilled to the bone. Men also lay down after a long march on wet ground and rolled up in soggy blankets. Common problems for McGuire and the doctors were coughs and respiratory ailments.

Filth was another problem. Sanitation was a serious issue. Many troops thought it was useless to build a latrine. They just relieved themselves wherever it was necessary. This naturally attracted flies and other vermin, which spread disease.

Mosquitoes were bad in the summertime, especially in July of 1862;[4] McGuire's friend, Sandie Pendleton, had to be sent home with the fever. The dreaded ailment gave the chills and the shakes. Some soldiers declared the mosquitoes formed into regiments and launched surprise attacks at night.

Fleas were bad, but body lice were worse.[5] Men nicknamed them "graybacks," "rebels," "tigers," and "Bragg's bodyguard."[6] The "graybacks" inspired many tall tales. One soldier wrote, "We all scratch alike, Generals and privates." The lack of body hygiene and warm or hot water contributed to this. In the Gettysburg campaign, men went weeks without a bath or a change of clothes. Even if they boiled their clothing in hot water, the bivouac area was still infested. So it was a continuous problem.

Always resourceful, the men in gray gave military terms to the methods of extermination. Killing of lice was referred to as "fighting under the black flag." Throwing away an infested shirt was "giving the vermin a parole." Sometimes the soldier turned the shirt inside out in an effort to get rid of the pesky critters. This was known as "executing a flank march."[7]

At the beginning of the war, soldiers were embarrassed or had feelings of disgrace when they became infected with body lice. As the war continued and the men became aware that this was a common problem, they joked about it. One soldier said he could not sleep soundly "unless I have a few graybacks gnawing on me."[8]

Many stories, similar to fish tales, developed. Several soldiers declared they had caught lice with the letters C.S. (Confederate States) on the backs. Another said he found a lice with the initials I.W. (In for the War). Others tried to manufacture the biggest lice. The best perhaps came from the lips of a soldier who said he saw his shirt moving. His first thought was that a rat was under his shirt. It was not a rat, but a big, fat lice.[9]

A lady from the rural area of Alabama sought to bring her children and visit the soldier-father in camp. Her husband advised against it saying, "If you was here the Boddy lice would eat up Booth of the children in one knight in spite of all we could doo; you dont have any idea what sort of animal they are."[10]

Private James Shields of the Virginia Light Artillery summarized the problem in a poem:

>Now I lay me down to sleep,
>While gray-backs oe'r my body creep;
>If I should die before I wake,
>I pray thee Lord their jaws to break.[11]

Water supply was another serious matter.[12] Troops usually drank whatever they could find. Often the water was polluted by animals, human waste, and other sources. The doctors took some of the blame for this, but they and the officers had a difficult time impressing upon the men the necessity of being careful.

Epidemics often struck the camps. Even childhood diseases visited the troops. One of the biggest causes of trouble was measles.[13] Rarely did measles prove fatal, but complications, resulting from troops returning to duty before they were fully recovered, led to fatalities. Measles struck hard in the winter. And malaria was the plague in the summer. A common question for the soldiers was "Have you had the shakes?" The next question, "How many times have you had the shakes?"[14]

"Smallpox, pneumonia, tuberculosis, and yellow fever all took a considerable toll of lives in both armies. But the principal killers were typhoid, and intestinal infections." The cases of typhoid cannot be documented because it is hard to determine what was typhoid, or what was camp fever. However, it does seem that one-fourth of all deaths from disease in Confederate ranks came from typhoid fever.[15] This illness hit its peak in the fall of 1861. There were less cases during the winter, but a sharp upswing every summer. During the first year of the war, one-fourth of all Union troops coming down with typhoid fever died. An Illinois soldier wrote in the autumn of 1861, "Tiford fever is Rageing here very much there has been several deaths of it." Another Union soldier declares, the fever patients "cannot be kept in their wretched bunks, but stagger about jabbering and muttering insanities till they lie down and die in their ragged, dirty uniforms...forty-two deaths in forty-two days."[16]

Compounding Dr. McGuire's problems was the fact that he never had medical facilities. Those coming on sick call were usually treated and then sent back to their tents or huts. Usually the best that Dr. McGuire had to use was a church or a large warehouse. He used the churches of Winchester in the winter of 1862 for hospital purposes, and he used a church in Port Republic during the Valley campaign. At Sharpsburg, he used a large farm.

There was also a problem of getting trained and qualified assistants, or male nurses. A key person was the hospital steward. This was a high-ranking noncommissioned officer. Generally, the individual held the rank of orderly sergeant. Normally, he had attended a medical school. Perhaps he had even graduated but had not completed all the requirements to be a doctor. Many times the steward had training in pharmacology.[17]

One of the main tasks of the steward was to supervise the maintenance and distribution of drugs, medical, and surgical supplies. If special foods, such as fruits or items such as tea, had been requisitioned for the care of the wounded, the steward was to insure that only the wounded obtained the special dietary items. The steward had the power to report even officers who gave him a difficult time.

The hospital clerk[18] was to handle all the paperwork and to keep up-to-date records for the doctor. Both the clerk and the steward were expected to be present at sick call each morning.

An important part of the hospital crew was the litter bearers.[19] The regimental band usually was detailed to infirmary duty. Later, 20 to 30 men were detailed from each regiment for this task. However, as battle and disease decimated the ranks, these numbers decreased.

## TRANSPORTATION

In the Civil War, men were transported to the hospitals in one of two ways, by the litter bearers or the ambulance service. There were stretchers,[20] but sometimes the men improvised. In one battle, a general officer suffered a stomach wound and was carried nearly a mile on a stretcher made by using two muskets and a blanket.[21]

The Union government issued 50,000 litters during the war of various types. One of the best weighed 24 pounds and had collapsible legs for storage when not in use. The men also used blankets with poles, as well as gates, ladders, and window shutters. Some even used the Indian method of the travois. The chair-seat method, often used by children to carry a playmate, was frequently used. Wounded, able to walk, were expected to make it on their own.

The Confederate Medical Service designated four ambulances to each regiment. Two of the horse-drawn vehicles had two wheels, and two of them had four wheels. "Both types left much to be desired." They were extremely uncomfortable. The wounded, jostled around by the springless carriages, often begged to be placed by the side of the road.[22] Some of McGuire's men were in the wagon train of misery leaving Gettysburg. The men had names for the ambulances. The two wheelers were called "the murderous twos," while the other was called "the merciful four."[23]

## EQUIPMENT

Hunter McGuire, like most physicians, had his own surgeon's kit. It contained two surgical saws, cutting pliers, a curved probe or retractor, clamps, a brush, and trepanning instruments. These items were carried in a wooden medical chest in his wagon.

At first, the regimental surgeon had only his "surgeon's field companion." This was supplemented by the orderly's "hospital knapsack." This item weighed about 20 pounds.

When the war began, officials were slow to adopt the idea of a hospital wagon. There were already too many wagons and horse-drawn vehicles connected with the army. The wagons were placed in the wagon train and that was usually too far to the rear to be of much assistance. The wagon carried a medicine chest, mess kit, and other hospital supplies.

For awhile panniers carrying the bare necessities were carried by pack mules.[24] Time proved the necessity for better methods, and special wagons were designed for the medical service.

As brigade surgeon, McGuire could be expected to have on hand:

| | |
|---|---|
| acetic acid | copaiba |
| adhesive plaster | creosote |
| alcohol | digitalis |
| aloes | ether |
| ammonia water | hydrochloric acid |
| arsenic oxide | hyoscyamus |
| assafoetida | morphine sulfate[25] |
| columbo | |

and, of course, opium, quinine sulphate, rhubarb, senna, sugar, and sulfuric acid.

# Chapter 7

Hunter McGuire and the other Confederate doctors wore a uniform much like that worn by other officers and men in gray. The cloth and cut of the uniform were the same. The facings though on the coat's collar and cuff, as well as the stripe down the sides of the trousers, were black. The infantry wore the light blue; the artillery, red; and the cavalry, buff or yellow. On the front of the cap were the letters "M. S." The letters were embroidered in gold and were embraced in two olive branches. McGuire, as the surgeon, had three rows of golden braid on the coat's sleeves, and a single star on each side of the coat's collar.[26] The medical service normally wore a green sash.[27]

The operating table was almost any table that could be found. At Antietam and elsewhere, kitchen tables were used. They were scrubbed down after an operation, usually with cold water. Cleanliness and sanitation were not the norm at that time.

## TREATMENT

The treatment of the wounded seems archaic and barbaric by today's standards. John W. Dyer, a Confederate soldier, writes of the medical treatment. "We had no anesthetic dressing then, and all the wounds were treated with the cold water treatment, which was to thickly bandage the wound and keep continually wet with cold water, till all signs of inflammation disappeared and the flesh began" to heal. Then the water was discontinued and dry bandages with salves and liniments substituted.

Gangrene often set in. Sometimes the decayed flesh was cut away. Another method was that of trying to burn it out with nitric acid. This was very painful and nerve-wracking. The acid was poured on the diseased part. The patient "saw smoke rise, the flesh sizzle and crisp up, with the patient screaming in agony."[28]

Morphine was given for pain; however, at times the supply was low. And during the Maryland campaign, those living near a church hospital in Keedysville had to keep their windows closed in an effort to escape the groans and screams of the wounded in the church.

Ninety-four percent of Civil War wounds came from Minié balls. "These soft lead missiles inflicted large and ragged wounds. They did more damage than the larger bullets of modern times."[29]

Perhaps it was due to the marksmanship or the lack of it, but the bulk of the Civil War wounds were arm and leg punctures. The *Medical and Surgical History* informs us that the wounds of the war could be listed as:

    10.77% facial and head wounds,
    18.37% of the trunk,
    35.71% of the upper extremities (shoulders, arms, and hands)
    35.15% of the lower extremities (hips, legs, and feet).

The most deadly wounds were those to the spine and abdomen. The rate of survival was very poor. The death rate from wounds was: spinal wounds, 55.5; abdomen, 48.7; pelvis, 29.7; head 28.9; lower extremities, 13.8; and upper extremities, 6.5.[30]

# Brigade Surgeon

The common treatment for diarrhea and dysentery were alternate doses of laxatives and opium. Confederate doctors often used derivatives of blackberry, willow, and sweetgum as astringents.

When battle loomed on the horizon, the brigade surgeon, on his own or in consultation with the division or corps medical director, had to make a selection of a site or sites for the field hospital. The site had to be near the line of battle, yet at least partially protected.[31] The Union hospitals at Antietam are a very good example of this. Most were within a mile or two of the action, yet behind the lee of a hill thus offering protection. Another key, essential element was water. At Antietam, the Hoffman and Poffenberger farms had excellent springs. There must be room for the ambulances to come and go, for men to be placed for treatment and for examination, and also a place for surgery. Protection, water, and space were of primary importance to the doctor in selecting a hospital along with easy accessibility.

In 1861, "the French army was considered the model army of the world." Yet an evaluation of that army showed a great need. The removal of the wounded from the battlefield and their transportation to the hospital are the most defective parts of the medical service. Even now,...this important service is delegated to no particular person...When the wounded fall in the ranks, there are none...to carry them off except their own comrades...[32] Sometimes five or six soldiers left their tasks to help a comrade to the rear, and rarely returned to the action.

The organization of the ambulance corps and medical attendants was a primary need. Doctors were too busy during the battle to direct the ambulances. Men needed to be designated and trained to assist the wounded from the field. Quick evacuation from the field of battle improved the chances for survival.

During the battle, the brigade surgeon was usually at the brigade hospital, directing the conduct of the hospital and supervising all the action. The entire medical staff was at work seeking to relieve the wounded.

As the ambulances or litter bearer brought the wounded in from the field of battle, there was a quick examination, and perhaps emergency treatment. "Amputations, resections of bone, ligatures of arteries," removals of shot and shell fragments, setting fractures, and major and minor operations were done as deemed necessary. The hospital staff tried to make the wounded comfortable.

Operations, even for general officers, were often performed by the light of a lamp. In fact, James P. Smith held the lamp for McGuire to operate on Jackson's arm at the Wilderness field hospital. At Antietam, a Union doctor was sure he would lose patients during the night because of the lack of light. Clara Barton saved the day when she arrived with many lamps.

Treatment was done in the open, in houses, barns, churches, and mills, or other old vacant buildings. When the action quieted, the wounds were dressed and reexamined. As soon as possible the wounded were taken by ambulance or train to a more permanent hospital or sent home to recover. For days, after Antietam, there were trains of horse-drawn ambulances leaving Sharpsburg, climbing South

Mountain, stopping for rest in Middletown, and then going on to Frederick. Some of the wounded were then placed in more permanent hospitals. Many times these were churches.

After a major battle, the surgeons were overwhelmed with work. There was little knowledge of antiseptic procedures. W. W. Keen wrote:

> We operated in old blood-stained and often puss-stained coats...with undisinfected hands...We used undisinfected instruments and marine sponges which had been used in prior pus cases and only washed in tap water.[33]

Surgeons probed for bullets with their fingers. Morphine was prescribed to ease pain, and efforts made to stop bleeding. Many times death occurred within three days of a wound, due primarily to bleeding or infection. Most of those who did not go home to recover from their wounds went to either Washington or Richmond. "The largest general hospital in the Confederacy was Chimborazo, located in Richmond. The doctor in charge was James B. McCaw. The hospital had 150 wards, and during the war treated 150,000." Chimborazo was "the first military hospital in point of size."[34]

Perhaps the best word to describe the dedicated Confederate surgeon would be "improvisation." The surgical achievements of both Confederate and Union surgeons, considering the general ignorance of antiseptic and other modern theories and methods, were deserving of much praise. Confederate surgeons, moreover, were especially handicapped by their overall lack of first-class surgical instruments. Surgeon Ferdinand E. Daniel, in a room lighted only by a smoky coal oil lamp, amputated a patient's hand with the contents of a small pocket case and a carpenter's saw. Another surgeon, confronted with a sudden and profuse secondary hemorrhage, successfully ligated the external carotid artery with the assistance of a pair of retractors improvised from the iron bale of a wooded water bucket.[35]

Dr. McGuire believed "that the adaptability of the Confederate surgeon to the emergencies of army life produced within their ranks some of the most proficient surgeons in the world, and, if these practitioners of wartime surgery are judged from the standpoint of their operative ingenuity and dexterity," then McGuire's praise is justified. He writes:

> The pliant bark of a tree made for him a good tourniquet; the juice of the green persimmon, a typtic; a knitting-needle, with its point sharply bent, a tenaculum, and a pen-knife in his hand, a scalpel and birtoury. I have seen him break off one prong of a common table-fork, bend the point of the other prong, and with it elevate the bone in depressed fracture of the skull and save life. Long before he knew the use of the porcelain-tipped probe for finding bullets, I have seen him use a piece of soft pine wood and bring it out of the wound marked by the leaden ball. Years before we were formally told of Nelaton's method of inverting the body in chloroform narcosis, I have seen it practiced by the Confederate surgeon....[36]

The improvision of the Confederate doctors is seen in some of the treatments they used:

| | |
|---|---|
| for burns | balsam or cucumbers |
| for colds | wild cherry or sugar from watermelon |
| for diarrhea | knob grass or rose geranium |
| for dysentery | blackberry roots or persimmons |
| for fever | jimson weed |
| for heart condition | jimson weed |
| for pneumonia | a mixture of opium, quinine, and brandy |
| for scurvy | watercress or wild yam[37] |

In 1861 many soldiers were presented with a copy of the *Soldier's Pocket Health Companion*—a book which listed 25 different items every soldier should have. Among them were:

6 linen pocket handkerchiefs
2–6 yards of white flannel
1 yard linen or muslin
1 pair of slippers
1 dozen court plasters
1 small box of lard
1 small bottle of Laudanum for diarrhea
1 small bottle of brandy
1 small bottle of peppermint
1 small bottle of camphor
1 paper cayenne pepper

# VIII

## Back to Winchester

For nearly two years Jackson was the key commander in the Valley and protector of Winchester. In time, "No city in the whole Confederacy loved Jackson more wholeheartedly, nor felt more deeply that he was its own particular savior...After all, Winchester, next to Lexington, was home...."[1]

"The country around Winchester—the gently rolling ridges, surmounted by groves of forest trees, the great North Mountains to the westward, rising sharply from the Valley, the cozy villages and comfortable farms, and in the clear blue distance to the south, the towering peaks of the Massanutten mountains is a picture not easily forgotten. And the little town, quiet and old fashioned, with its ample gardens, and red bricked pavements, is not unworthy of its surroundings."[2]

Winchester was a theater of operations for most of the war. One source says the city changed hands 76 times. Three major battles were fought around the city, and skirmishes were too numerous to mention. McGuire's family lived through these days and shared the alarm and trauma of those moments in Winchester and the Shenandoah Valley.

Jackson was supposed to leave the Centreville-Manassas area on November 4, 1861, to go to Winchester. Early in the morning the various officers of the brigade visited with the general. In the afternoon, the command was formed behind the bivouac area of the Second Virginia, McGuire's old unit. Jackson made a very moving speech to the men, one that caused tears to run down their cheeks. Jackson stood in his stirrups, raised his hands to the troops, and in a voice charged with emotion, concluded his address:

> In the Army of the Shenandoah, you see the First Brigade! In the Army of the Potomac you were the First Brigade! In the Second Corps of this army you were the First Brigade! You are the First Brigade in the affections of your general, and I hope by your future deeds and bearing you will be handed down to posterity as the First Brigade in this, our second War of Independence. Farewell![3]

There was a momentary quietness. Then men started to cheer, and soon the roar of voices "shook the countryside." Jackson deeply moved, unwilling to trust his emotions, waved his cap and rode off.

Once reaching Winchester, Jackson was appalled by the needs of his new command. He telegraphed the government in Richmond and asked for reinforcements, including his old brigade.

On November 7 the First Brigade was ordered to Winchester. A pouring rain on the eighth could not dampen the spirits of the men as they marched to board trains for the West. They were returning to their beloved commander.

The cold and drafty freight cars took the men to Strasburg, where they disembarked and started marching in the sun for Winchester. The sun dried the wet uniforms and helped dry out the mud. Dr. McGuire soon had his hands full with many men on sick call.[4] Getting soaking wet and riding in the railroad cars brought influenza, measles, and other diseases to the troops.

The First Brigade was happy to be in Winchester, and the townspeople rejoiced to see them. Some of the women said they had no fear of the Yankees now that the "Stonewall Men" were present.

Jackson and McGuire had much in common in their love for the Shenandoah Valley. Mrs. Jackson writes:

> General Jackson was so captivated with the Valley of Virginia, the more he saw of it in his campaigns, that he used to say that when the war was over he wanted to have a home in the Shenandoah Valley, and there indulge his taste for rural pursuits, and enjoy the domestic life which was so dear to him. The beauty and grandeur of the scenery, with its chains of mountains, limpid streams, fine forests, dales and fertile fields, were to him charming beyond description.[5]

Jackson established his headquarters in a home just north of the McGuire residence on Braddock Street. Writing to Mrs. Jackson he said:

> This house belongs to Lieutenant Colonel Moore of the Fourth Virginia Volunteers, and has a large yard around it. The situation is beautiful. The building is of cottage style and contains six rooms....Through the blessing of our ever-kind Heavenly Father, I am quite comfortable.[6]

Located between the Moore home and the McGuire residence was the Presbyterian manse and the home of Dr. James Graham.

In December, Jackson was able to secure a pass for his wife, Mary Anna, to join him in Winchester. Arriving late one evening, she stayed at the Hotel Taylor[7] and then went to Jackson's headquarters for the rest of the month.

Large groups of soldiers posed health problems for McGuire. Bad weather, poor sanitary conditions, and the lack of good food and quarters, brought epidemics that spilled over to the residents of Winchester. Dr. McGuire had to treat soldiers and civilians for typhoid, dysentery, and other ailments. Scarlet fever and diptheria took a heavy toll among the very young and the elderly.

The citizens of Winchester offered their homes to house the troops; however, Jackson refused this offer. The men were soldiers and had to stay in camp. A site was selected four and a half miles north of Winchester on the Stephenson Road. The camp was called "New Centerville." In spite of Jackson's orders and guards, the troops found ways to enter Winchester to find companionship and drink.

December 1861 was spent in drilling and in forays against Dam No. 5 on the Chesapeake and Ohio Canal. Jackson's objective was to disrupt the shipping of coal and produce from Cumberland, Maryland, to Washington, D.C. Dr. McGuire's task here was to help the soldiers with frostbite or overexposure. Some of them worked in the cold waters of the Potomac trying to destroy the canal.

The War Department sent six thousand troops commanded by Brigadier General William W. Loring as reinforcements to Jackson. The entire command suffered from the cold as there were not enough coats and blankets. The men shivered in their tents and by their campfires.

The Confederate troops hoped to go into winter quarters in Winchester. General Jackson had other plans. He believed that campaigning was healthier than being in camp. Jackson hoped to capture Romney, and take control of the strategic area to the west. Therefore, at three o'clock in the afternoon of December 31, 1861, the men were told to draw rations and be ready to move out in 12 hours.

The cold abated and the weather became springlike. Jackson headed for Bath (now Berkeley Springs), hoping to force the evacuation of Hancock, Maryland. This movement would split the Union forces under Colonel John Reese Kenly in Romney, causing it to be evacuated by the Union forces.

The lovely afternoon weather turned colder by evening. The supply wagons could not keep up with the troops. Coats and blankets had been piled in the wagons along with the rations. A blizzard developed making the men miserable. Brigadier General Loring's men thought Jackson was crazy, but they plodded on in the cold, wind, and snow.[8]

These conditions lasted until January 3 when the wagons finally arrived. But Jackson wanted to keep moving and would not permit the men to cook their rations.

Bath was captured, and Hancock was shelled. But more suffering was ahead as the men headed for their last objective, Romney. The route that Jackson's men took was rugged with sharp curves in the road. One of the heaviest snowfalls in memory blanketed the area. The men and wagons struggled ahead with great difficulty. Jackson even put his shoulder to the wheel of a wagon stuck in the snow.

Seven days later the First Brigade entered Romney. A high wind and sleet made it difficult for the men and animals to stand. McGuire treated a lot of men for bruises and some for fractured bones. The troops looked like snowmen, coated with ice and with icicles hanging from caps and eyelashes. Nearly one-third of the command was unable to keep up, and the Rockbridge Artillery took refuge in a church. The men were exhausted.

Stonewall Jackson had pushed his men to the limits of their endurance. The First Brigade was ordered back to Winchester. Soon that city was full of men with pneumonia and severe colds. There were a lot of deaths. Most of the men had suffered frostbite, necessitating many amputations.[9] McGuire had more opportunities to practice surgery than he desired.

The retreat from Romney was terrible. The men endured mud, sleet, and snow. A bitter wind arose that chilled the men to the bone. Near dusk, a courier was sent ahead to look for a farmhouse where Jackson and the staff could obtain something to eat.

A place was found, and a considerate host spread a substantial meal. One of the younger officers produced a bottle of whiskey. Following military protocol, he asked General Jackson if he might not like a drink to help warm him. Jackson turned to Dr. McGuire, who was seated by his side, and said, "Dr. McGuire, do you think it would do me good?" Hunter McGuire replied, "Yes." Jackson, being inexperienced at this sort of thing, took the bottle and poured a tumbler half full of whiskey without adding any water. He drank several large gulps.[10]

When the staff finished the meal, they thanked their hosts and remounted to continue the journey. Jackson showed no effects from the whiskey, other than being warm. Soon after they started to ride he unbuttoned his coat, threw back the flaps, and began to open his shirt. Dr. McGuire, of course, protested. "General, you will take cold. The weather is very bitter." Jackson replied, "No, Dr. McGuire, the weather is moderating."[11]

The men felt that the Romney expedition had ended in failure. But Jackson did not think so. He had endured the hardships along with his men. The general had to cover 40 miles of mountain road to reach Winchester. So when he dropped in unexpectedly at the Reverend Graham's, the pastor and Jackson's wife were surprised and overjoyed to see him. The fire and the winter evening were delightful. Jackson said, "This is the very essence of comfort."[12] The general was back in the Valley, back in Winchester.

In February 1862, McGuire kept busy with cases much like those in his prewar medical practice. Common colds, influenza, and pneumonia were prevalent. When he found any spare time, Hunter ministered to the townspeople too. There is a possibility that McGuire lived part of the time at home, and then made his rounds of the various hospitals located in the churches and warehouses of Winchester. Each morning after sick call, McGuire went to Jackson's headquarters on Braddock Street to report on the medical condition of the army.

Dr. James Graham was very much impressed with the former teacher from the Virginia Military Institute. He was one of the most devout, humble, and sincere Christians he had ever met. The parson did not consider him odd or aloof. To Dr. Graham, Jackson was..."just a simple gentleman, such as we meet in large numbers every day upon our streets, and whom we salute without once thinking whether there is anything peculiar about them. He was a shy, reserved family man and a Christian."[13] Perhaps that is one of the best descriptions ever given of Jackson.

The Graham residence was the home away from home for the Jacksons. The general and his wife had a room upstairs and one down. Meals were eaten with the Grahams and the two families became very close friends.

Describing the winter of 1863, Anna Jackson wrote, "We spent as happy a winter as ever falls to the lot of mortals on this earth."[14]

The staff members also had a little break. In the winter evenings McGuire and his young friends, Henry Douglas and Sandie Pendleton, paid visits to the homes of the young ladies of Winchester. McGuire probably made quite a few introductions.

During the day the troops were drilled in the fields near the edge of town. Jackson was preparing them for the action that was sure to come when spring arrived. Near the end of February, Jackson eased up a bit and permitted the enlisted men to visit Winchester. Many of the young soldiers from the Deep South enjoyed their first snowball fights, sleigh rides, and taffy pulls. Colonel Pendleton erected a 60- by 25-foot chapel. There was good attendance—the prospect of battle, death, and the realization that the general expected the men to go to church provided additional motivation.

The high waters of the Potomac and the cold winds of winter held the Union forces in camp during February. But late in the month, President Lincoln gave the orders for a general advance. When the month of March arrived, Jackson's men and the people of Winchester realized that it was just a matter of time before the men in blue advanced.

In early March, Union General Nathaniel P. Banks left his winter quarters around Frederick, Maryland, and marched to Harpers Ferry. His objective was Winchester.

To meet the threat, Jackson told Major John Harman, his quartermaster officer, to establish a supply base south of Winchester. Mrs. Jackson packed her baggage and headed south for a safer area. A year would pass before she would see her husband again.

By March 11, the advancing Union column was within four miles of Winchester. From scouts, Jackson realized that he was outnumbered seven to one. Yet, he was ready to give battle. In the evening, Jackson called a council of war and discussed the situation with the five regimental commanders of the Stonewall Brigade.

Fear must have already stricken the officers or else they felt a tactical withdrawal was the only answer. They had already started their baggage trains south. Jackson was reluctant to "abandon a single acre of his beloved Valley to the enemy." Although he considered a surprise attack, he realized his position was untenable.

Jackson ordered the baggage, supply, and medical wagons south. The sick were to go to Staunton, while the other wagons were headed to Mount Jackson, the place selected by Major Harman. Jackson then called for a time of prayer. Finally, Jackson said, "I must retreat and wait for a better time."

The general went to the Graham's home and bade a hasty, sad farewell. Then, he and McGuire rode southward through the streets of Winchester. They trotted along on the Valley Pike and headed for Newtown (now Stephens City). McGuire relates:

(Reaching a high point,) we both turned to look at Winchester, just evacuated and now left to the mercy of the Federal soldiers. I think that a man may sometimes yield to an overwhelming emotion, and I was utterly overcome by the fact that I was leaving all that I held dear on earth. But my emotion was arrested by one look at Jackson. His face was fairly blazing with the fire that was burning in him, and I felt awed before him. Presently he cried out with a manner almost savage, 'That is the last council of war I will ever hold!' And it was—his first and last.[15]

# IX

# The Valley Campaign

Less than two weeks after McGuire and Jackson shared the sad retreat on the Valley Pike, Jackson was back at Kernstown, two miles south of Winchester. Jackson had learned that General Banks had taken his army to Manassas to prevent an approach on Washington from that direction. Therefore, Jackson decided to return to the Winchester area. At Kernstown, he encountered seven thousand Union soldiers under General James Shields. Jackson's command suffered heavy losses and met the only defeat of his brilliant military career.

Although heavily outnumbered, Jackson's men fought valiantly behind stonewalls and natural defensive barriers. They remained until their ammunition was depleted. Seeing their plight, General Richard B. Garnett, one of Jackson's subordinates, gave the order to retreat. This infuriated Jackson who wanted to strike the Union forces with the bayonet.[1]

Despite the retreat, Kernstown was a small engagement with big results. It struck fear into the hearts of the Northern government. They did not know when or where Stonewall Jackson might strike next. Therefore, thousands of Union soldiers were placed at strategic locations to prevent a surprise attack.

Jackson left a small force to keep Shields busy. That may not have been necessary. Residents of Winchester reported Union soldiers running through the streets of the town toward the rear while the fighting was going on. Some Northern newspapers reported the South would have won at Kernstown had they been able to stay on the field another 10 minutes.

As Jackson's troops were falling back, Dr. McGuire reported that a lot of time would be required to remove the wounded, and he asked the general, "Can you protect us?"

Jackson looked at McGuire and replied, "Make yourself easy about that. This army stays until the last wounded man is removed. Before I will leave them to the enemy I will lose more men.[2]

A chilling rain fell through the night as the ambulance crews used the eerie lights of their lanterns to search for the wounded. The rain washed some of the blood from the earth.

In a few days, Dr. McGuire received the news that his sister, Mary, was very ill with tuberculosis and was growing rapidly worse. Knowing Jackson's plan to move to the New Market area, 50 miles away, McGuire went to the general with a request. Jackson said, "I can't give you permission to go (into Winchester) but if you go, please wear your sash."[3] So Hunter dressed in full uniform and wore his green medical sash.

Riding to the outskirts of his beloved hometown, McGuire concealed his horse in the cellar of a friend and then made his way through the alleys and back streets of Winchester until he reached home. Hunter talked with his mother and with Mary and did what he could to make her comfortable. Some of his comrades had taken up a collection, so Dr. McGuire left the money with his mother to help meet expenses. Throughout the war, these funds helped to meet her needs.[4] She was always grateful for the money her son brought at the secret meeting.

They headed south in the rain and mud back to camp. Governor Letcher had called out all the militia during the Union advance on Winchester. Among those marching from Augusta County to join Jackson's army was Jedediah Hotchkiss, a self-made engineer and map maker.

T. Harry Williams, a great student of the Civil War, calls Hotchkiss "perhaps the foremost mapper of the war." At least half of the Confederate maps in the *Atlas of the Official Records* were drawn by Hotchkiss. Jed became an aide and courier to Jackson. "But essentially he was an engineer and the best topographical engineer in the Confederate Army. He was the man more responsible than any other for Jackson's ability to proceed in sure knowledge of the terrain." Hotchkiss became an extremely valuable addition to Jackson's staff, and in time, one of Hunter McGuire's best friends.[5]

Jackson and Hotchkiss met at Narrow Passage on March 26, 1862. The general said to Jed, "I want you to make me a map of the Valley from Harpers Ferry to Lexington, showing all the points of offense and defense between those points. Mr. Pendleton will give orders for whatever outfit you want."[6]

Hotchkiss kept a journal throughout the war and made many interesting notes. Amount them were these comments about the staff.

> I am very much pleased with General Jackson and his staff. He is at times very chatty, but usually has little to say. Sunday he went through one of his brigades with a bundle of tracts and distributed them. He stays to himself most of the time; eats very sparingly; does not drink coffee or tea and eats scarcely any meat...Lieutenant A. S. Pendleton,...is a young man of about twenty-two and light haired. He graduated at Washington College and has taught in Lexington. He was at the University of Virginia when the war broke out. He is talented, an admirable talker, and a man of fine sense and acquirements...Dr. Hunter McGuire, the Medical Director, is also a young man of fine talents. He is not more than twenty-six, but has been a

professor...He is the son of Dr. (Hugh) McGuire of Winchester, of whom you have often heard. The Doctor is one of my brother George's sort of men, blunt, good humored and full of honest life...Lieutenant Henry Kyd Douglas is from Maryland...He is quite young, but has been practicing law in St. Louis. He is one of your wide awake, smart young men. I like him too.[7]

Throughout the war, McGuire was concerned about things in Winchester and what was happening to his friends and to his family. Letters arrived in camp on March 27, saying the women of Winchester had buried the dead from the fields of Kernstown, and that Confederate prisoners being marched through Winchester defiantly cheered for President Jefferson Davis.[8] Union soldiers were searching private homes and insulting the women.

The early part of April found McGuire with the rest of Jackson's staff at the home of the widow Steenbergen near Rude's Hill,[9] north of New Market. The heavy rains and lack of shelter caused a lot of sickness, and once again Dr. McGuire was very busy.

Jackson knew that a Union force was preparing to move against him from the west, and he knew that additional troops were in Winchester. His theory, however, was "never take counsel of your fears...Always mystify, mislead, and surprise the enemy."[10] The next six weeks were to be a model of this type of action, and McGuire was a part of it.

With the help of his maps, his staff, his troops, and "Almighty God," Jackson made the Shenandoah Valley his ally. He used the woods, hills, mountains, and hidden trails to hide his movements and deceive his enemy. The Shenandoah was "a lovely Valley to fight for,"[11] and Jackson did his best.

Meanwhile, Major General Richard S. Ewell's division was sent to reinforce Jackson. Richard Taylor, the son of former president Zachary Taylor, commanded the Louisiana infantry in Ewell's command. Crossing Swift Run Gap, the troops moved to Conrad's Store (modern-day Elkton).

Taylor was as impressed with the view as Jackson and McGuire must have been.

> The great Valley of Virginia was before us in all its beauty. Fields of wheat spread far and wide, interspersed with woodlands, bright in their robes of tender green. Wherever appropriate sites existed, quaint old mills, with turning wheels, were busy grinding the previous year's harvest, and grove and eminence showed comfortable homesteads...The theatre of war in this region was from Staunton to the Potomac, one hundred and twenty miles, with an average width of some twenty-five miles; and the Blue Ridge and Alleghenies bounded it east and west. Drained by the Shenandoah with its numerous affluents, the surface was nowhere flat, but a succession of graceful swells, occasionally rising into abrupt hills...Frequent passes or gaps in the mountains through which wagon roads had been constructed, afforded easy access from east and west; and pikes were excellent, though unmetaled roads became heavy with rains.[12]

# The Valley Campaign

Jackson left Ewell's men at Conrad's Store to check a possible advance by Union General Banks. On April 30, in a driving rain, Jackson began withdrawing southward, turning east in the process. Banks reported that Jackson was abandoning the Shenandoah Valley and heading for Richmond.

Jackson had other plans. At Mechum's Station, his men boarded a train and started westward. They were very much surprised to find their destination was Staunton. Soon Jackson linked up with Brigadier General Edward Johnson. Near McDowell on May 7–8, Jackson routed Union forces under General Robert H. Milroy. In the process, he suffered 498 casualties. With the Union retreat, Jackson wired Richmond, "God blessed our arms with victory." Then he turned east toward the center of the Shenandoah Valley. With the one Union army out of the way, he could now concentrate on Banks.

By May 20, Jackson and Ewell had joined forces at New Market. Crossing the Massanutten Mountains (a 50-mile stretch running north and south in the middle of the Valley), Jackson headed for the Luray Valley. The objective was Front Royal. Once this was in Confederate hands, Jackson would have an excellent route to the flank and rear of the Union army, and the opportunity to reach Winchester.

On the march to Front Royal, Jackson encountered Belle Boyd, the famous spy, who gave him information as to the location and number of Union forces in the town.

Friday, May 23, was clear and hot. As the dawn broke, the town was in the hands of the First Maryland Infantry (Union) commanded by Colonel John R. Kenly. Suddenly from the hills and woods surrounding the town emerged Jackson's gray-clad columns, including the First Maryland Infantry, C.S.A. The Union forces were overwhelmed, although they offered strong resistance at Guard Hill north of town. Kenly's command retreated to Cedarville, three miles north, and Front Royal was occupied by the Confederates. Jackson's foot cavalry pressed on and destroyed the Union forces, capturing six hundred prisoners. He lost but 50 men. The road to Winchester was now open.

Although little information is available, it seems that with the rapid movement of Jackson's troops, Dr. McGuire checked the wounded, and then left them in local hospitals set up for those who fell at McDowell and at Front Royal.

Union General Banks at Strasburg, Virginia, was now in great danger. Not until 3 A.M. on the twenty-fourth did he start to send his sick and wounded northward toward Winchester. The main body of troops did not start until mid-morning. By that time it was too late. Jackson's men were coming fast. Panic swept the Union ranks. Wagon drivers smashed into each other. Ambulances upset along the road. The men in blue wanted to get to Winchester before Jackson. Jackson, of course, wanted to prevent them from reaching Winchester. The Union retreat became a rout, and six miles of the roadside became littered with equipment and supplies.

Although they were well-disciplined troops, Jackson's men had a momentary lapse as they gathered food, supplies, and military equipment from the roadside.[13] The slight delay gave Banks' command the time to reach Winchester.

Banks thought he would be safe. However, he underestimated the man they called Stonewall.

By midnight, Banks realized Jackson had no intention of stopping his pursuit, so he ordered what was left of his trains northward to the Potomac at Williamsport, Maryland. His wagons were still moving through the streets of Winchester when Jackson launched his attack at daybreak.

The first battle of Winchester, McGuire's hometown, was under way. Jackson's plan was simple. Ewell would attack the Union left, a portion of his own command would hold the center, and the other Confederate troops would turn the Union right and rush into Winchester.

General Ewell encountered heavy opposition in his front. But on the right, the Confederates brushed aside the Union opposition. For three hours Banks held on. Then, Jackson launched one of his famous flanking movements. The Union line was broken, and Jackson ordered his entire line forward. The Confederate line surged forward in triumph. The blue-clad infantry swarmed through the street of Winchester like a panic-stricken mob.

Banks tried to stop the retreat, yelling at some of his men, "Stop, men! Don't you love your country."

One Union soldier never stopped running, but yelled at his general, "Yes,...and I'm trying to get to it just as fast as I can."

The men in blue ran to Martinsburg and then on to Williamsport. Some covered 35 miles in 14 hours. They suffered from blistered feet. Banks lost 3,030 men of the 8,500 in his command. He lost so much of his equipment and supplies that the grateful Confederates gave him the nickname, "Commissary Banks."[14]

May 25 was a great day in Winchester—the Yankees had been driven from the town, and Jackson and the men from the Valley were back. Old men and ladies, little children, the rich and poor rushed into the street to greet the ragged soldiers who had delivered them from the hand of the enemy. Food was distributed, and all looked for friends and loved ones. "Windows and doors, closed for months were thrown open." There were tears and smiles. The reception for Jackson and his men is beyond description. "They (the people of Winchester) convinced him that they were 'worth fighting for.'"[15]

Dr. McGuire was glad to be home and he was elated "because we have captured more medical stores than those in the whole Confederacy."[16] For many months these captured supplies were used by McGuire to meet the medical needs of Jackson's command.

One of the few McGuire reports, surviving the war, reads:

> One of the largest storehouses in the town had been appropriated by the United States Medical Service purveyor and filled with medicines, instruments and hospital stores. The supply was very large and intended for the armies under the command of General Shields and Frémont, as well as that of General Banks....[17]

Jackson's army had cleared the Shenandoah Valley, recaptured Winchester, along with over 9,000 small arms, plus 500,000 rounds of ammunition. Cattle, bacon, bread, sugar, and salt supplies were also among the spoils of victory.[18] The hungry Confederates feasted on the supplies "Commissary Banks" had so graciously left behind.

Monday, May 26, was set aside as a day of Thanksgiving, and the chaplains conducted services at 4 P.M.

The battle of Winchester had special significance for Dr. McGuire. Some Union physicians were captured, seven of them were unconditionally released by McGuire with Jackson's consent. These men were to report to the Secretary of War in Washington and urge the release of all captured Confederate medical officers. Soon all doctors captured in the war and imprisoned by both sides "were released and returned to their respective commands." Several times during the war, this plan was altered by political events and red tape. But whenever McGuire had the opportunity, he released the captive Union doctors.

This action by McGuire was credited by at least two sources as being the forerunner of the Red Cross. Dr. Josiah F. Day, Jr., states, "The initiative in instituting the practice of free discharge of surgeons belongs to General Jackson and his chief surgeon, Hunter McGuire."[19]

A year later, at a meeting of the Association of the Medical Officers of the Army and Navy of the Confederacy, Dr. E. D. Newton of Georgia read a paper on the beginning of the Red Cross. He said:

> Before the Red Cross Society was organized the ideas of the Red Cross Society were first put into practice by Dr. Hunter McGuire, chief surgeon and medical director of Jackson's corps....This human and generous action by Dr. McGuire and his commander was, however, the first practical operation of the views and suggestions of this noble Swiss gentleman, (M. Henry Dunant) which culminated in his full organization of the Red Cross Society of Geneva, Switzerland, in 1864.[20]

One scholar writes, "He humanized war by originating the custom of releasing all medical officers immediately after they were captured."[21]

While McGuire remained in Winchester, taking inventory of his acquired supplies, Jackson threatened Harpers Ferry. He had to withdraw when he learned that the Lincoln government was trying to catch him in a three-pronged movement, cutting him off at Strasburg. Thus, a forceful march south was begun with Jackson eluding the snare. In five days he was near Harrisonburg, and then proceeded east toward Port Republic.

Sadness struck the army as General Turner Ashby, the cavalry chieftain, was killed in fighting near Harrisonburg on June 6. Jackson wept when he heard the news.

Jackson hated profanity. At Winchester he berated General Richard Taylor for swearing while cheering his men forward. On another occasion McGuire was treating Major Harman, the quartermaster of the army. Jackson enquired of his health. He said, "Doctor, how is Major Harman today?"

Hunter said, "He must be better, for he is swearing again. 'General Jackson gave Harman such a lecture the next day that Colonel Pendleton advised me to keep out of Harman's way, as he swore he was going to shoot me.'"[22]

McGuire also felt Jackson's wrath. While moving some wounded from a church at Port Republic, Union artillery started to fire on the church, scaring the ambulance drivers. Hunter relates:

> I was riding up and down the line of ambulances and wagons, swearing at the men in a right lively manner. I didn't know that General Jackson was within a mile of me, when I felt his hand upon my shoulder and he quietly asked me: "Doctor, don't you think they could get along without swearing?"[23]

Jackson had immobilized the army under General Nathaniel Banks. Now he had to contend with Union General John C. Frémont's troops coming from the west, and those under General James Shields who had reoccupied Front Royal. Whether it was fear or an error in leadership, or a combination of both, it took Frémont's command eight days to cover 70 miles. At the same time, Jackson's "foot cavalry" were marching 50 miles in two days.

Jackson was characterized by audacity. And even with two Union armies closing in on him, he waited, confident of repelling them. He was with the main body of his command at Port Republic, while Ewell was four miles northwest at the hamlet of Cross Keys.

This would be Jackson's fourth battle on the Sabbath. First, there was Manassas, then Kernstown, Winchester, and on June 8, 1862, Cross Keys. Frémont's army came out from Harrisonburg, 10,000 strong. Ewell faced him with six thousand men. Frémont seemed to be more afraid of losing the battle than anxious to win. He committed but five of his 24 regiments. These were rolled back by a Confederate counterattack under Brigadier General Isaac R. Trimble. Cross Keys was a minor battle, 684 Union casualties, and 284 Confederate. However, the Union army under Frémont was no longer a threat.

Monday, June 9, brought the battle of Port Republic. Union forces under Shields advanced from the Luray Valley. They had handled Jackson at Kernstown, so they came with confidence. The fighting was severe, indeed the heaviest of the Valley campaign. Jackson lost eight hundred of the 5,900 men engaged in the action. Had Frémont attacked from the west, Jackson would have been in great danger. But by the end of the day, both Shields and Frémont were in retreat. The Valley campaign was over.

A New York cavalrymen wrote home saying "It cannot be denied that this Jackson is a man of decided genius, and that very few in our army are fit to compete with him."

The Valley campaign is "a model example of how to get the most from the least. A quiet gentleman from Lexington—an unpretentious officer who persistently sucked lemons and spoke little—had saved Richmond and preserved his beloved Valley through a series of some of the most extraordinary movements in military annals."[24]

A Richmond writer inquired of McGuire, "What do you think, Doctor, was Jackson's greatest feat?"

# The Valley Campaign

McGuire replied, "I think his greatest feat was his Valley Campaign. He had in the Valley about 15,000 men...the Federals between 50,000 and 70,000. Milroy was at Shenandoah Mountain, Banks was near Winchester, Shields was about Manassas, and McDowell was west of the Valley. He so divided and engaged these different forces armies as nearly always when he met them to be the stronger party and whipped them in detail."[25]

McGuire's problems during the Valley campaign were with fatigue and sore feet. The constant movement took their toll. A listing of the movements in 1862 shows:

| | |
|---|---|
| May 8 | The battle of McDowell |
| May 23 | Front Royal |
| May 24 | Middletown |
| May 25 | Winchester |
| June 6 | Turner Ashby killed |
| June 8 | Cross Keys |
| June 9 | Port Republic |

This amounted to 676 miles in 48 days, a tremendous feat. McGuire and Jackson both realized there was a limit to human endurance. And for a few days, the army rested at Weyers Cave, south of Port Republic. The respite was short. General George B. McClellan was advancing on Richmond, and once again Jackson's army was needed in the east.

From the Valley campaign, a prize possession came to Dr. McGuire. On one of the battlefields, a supply of swords, some of them with golden engravings, were captured. They were brought to Jackson, as such items were to be turned over to the commanding officer. One sword was especially fine, and had a M.S. (Medical Service) engraving. This sword, Jackson presented to his brigade surgeon. Dr. McGuire gave the sword to his mother for safekeeping during the war. She hid it under the mattress. The sword was thus preserved and remains to this day in the possession of the McGuire family.[26]

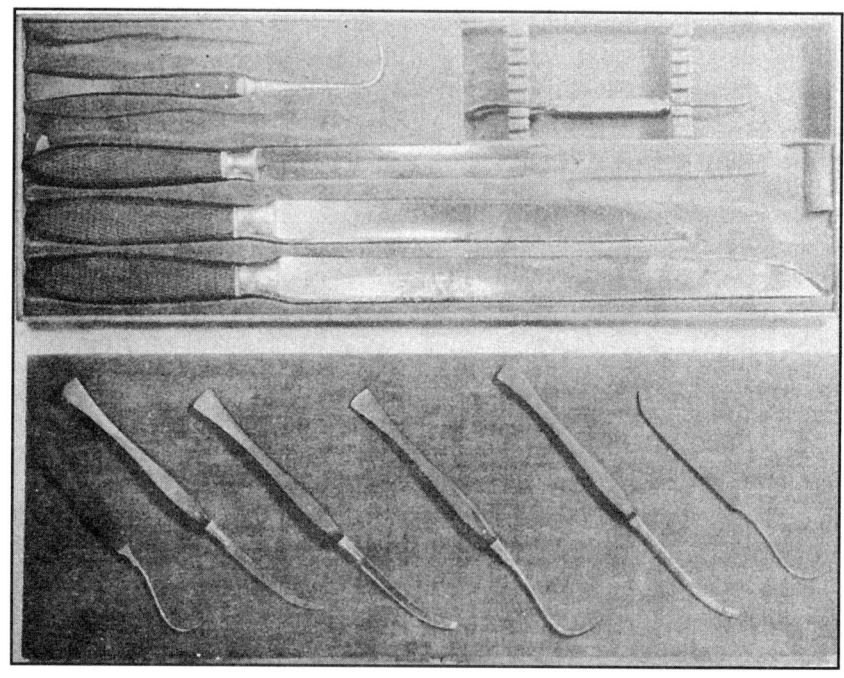

*A Surgeon's Kit*

U.S. Army Medical Museum

*A Civil War Ambulance*

U.S. Army Medical Museum

*Samuel Preston Moore,
Surgeon General
of the Confederacy*
Library of Congress

*Alexander Swift
"Sandie" Pendleton*
Southern Historical Society
Collection, Chapel Hill, North Carolina

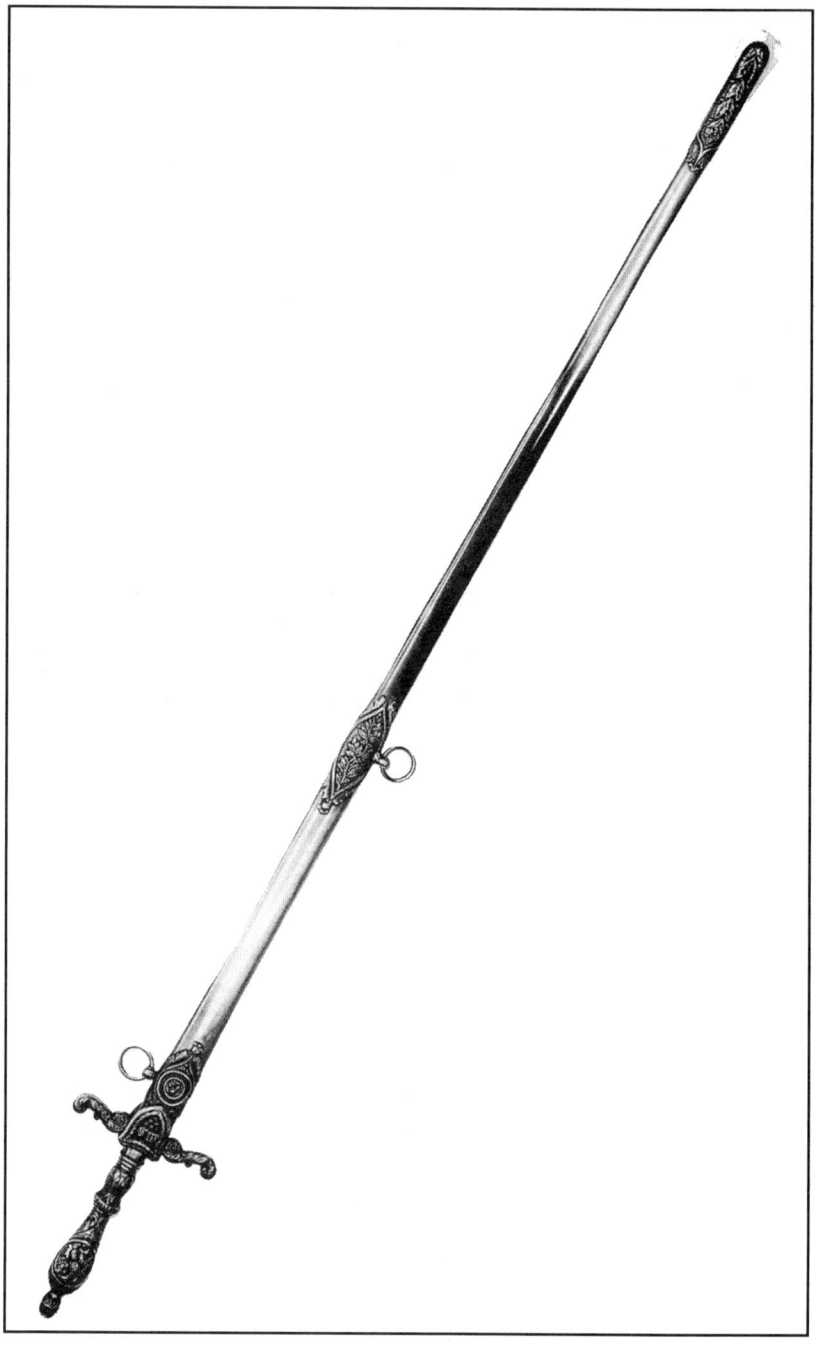

*Stonewall Jackson Presented This Sword to Dr. Hunter McGuire*

Courtesy of the McGuire Family

*Staff of Lieutenant General Thomas J. "Stonewall" Jackson*
Virginia Military Institute Archives

*The Deathbed of Stonewall Jackson in the Chandler House*
Author's Collection

The Winchester Portrait
Lieutenant General Thomas J. "Stonewall" Jackson

*Guiney's Station, Virginia*
*Last words of Thomas Jonathan Jackson: "Let us cross over the river, and rest under the shade of the trees."*

Author's Collection

*Jedediah Hotchkiss, Topographical Engineer of the Army of Northern Virginia*
Library of Congress

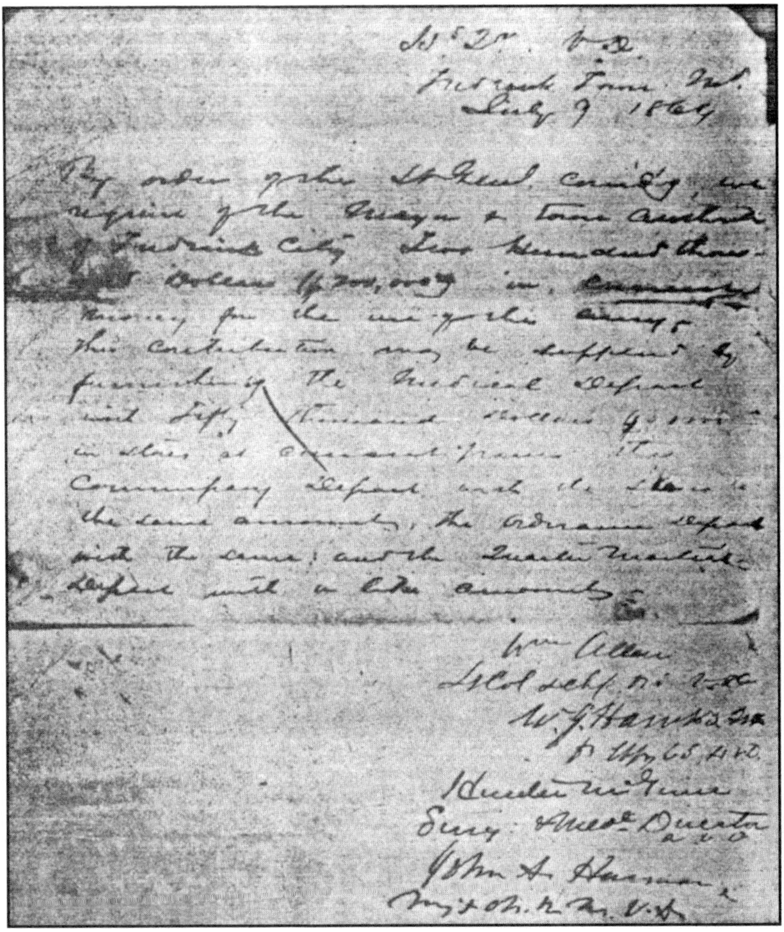

Hd Qrs V.D.
Frederick Town Md.
July 9 1864

By order of the Lt. Genl. Comdg, we require of the Mayor & town authorities of Frederick City Two Hundred Thousand Dollars ($200,000) in current money for the use of this army.
This contribution may be supplied by furnishing the Medical Depart with fifty thousand dollars ($50,000) in stores at current prices; the Commissary Depart with the stores to the same amount; the Ordnance Depart with the same; and the Quarter Master Depart with a like amount.

Wm Allan
Lt Col & Chf. Ord. V.D.
W. J. Hawks Maj
& Chf. Comy. V.D.
Hunter McGuire
Surg. & Med. Director
V.D.
John A. Harman
Maj & Ch. Qr. Mr. V.D.

*A Ransom Note to the City of Frederick, Maryland, from Jubal Early, July 9, 1864*
City of Frederick, Maryland

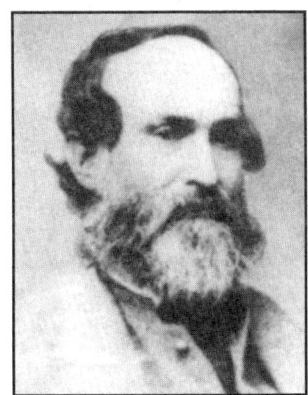

*General Jubal A. Early*
Library of Congress

*Grave of Captain Hugh Holmes McGuire, Brother of Hunter Holmes McGuire*

Author's Collection

*Mary Stuart Married Hunter Holmes McGuire, December 19, 1866*

Courtesy of the McGuire Family

*Virginia Hospital, Richmond, Virginia*

Virginia Historical Society

*Doctors and Nurses at St. Luke's Home for the Sick*
Virginia Historical Society

*Dr. Hunter McGuire Lecturing to Staff*
Virginia Historical Society

*Grave of Dr. Hunter Holmes McGuire, Hollywood Cemetery*

Virginia Historical Society

*St. Luke's Hospital, Richmond, Virginia*
Courtesy of St. Luke's Hospital and Dr. John Lynch

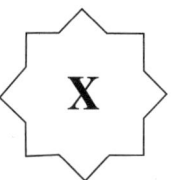

# The Summer of 1862

Jackson's command headed east from Weyers Cave to assist Lee's troops in the defense of Richmond. Sandie Pendleton, James Boswell, Henry Douglas, Stapleton Crutchfield,[1] and Dr. McGuire rode through Albemarle and Louisa Counties. The countryside was pretty. No Yankees were in pursuit. The young and dashing men were part of the great Stonewall's staff. At the end of each day they looked for "lighted parlors" and a welcome "by pretty girls and merry music." The trip to Gordonsville "was a little holiday,"[2] a lighter moment in the darkness of war.

Jackson was not very successful in his part of the Seven Days' or Peninsula campaign. He was not familiar with the terrain. The doctors of our era maintain that he was suffering from exhaustion, stemming from the Valley campaign, and from riding over one hundred miles in less than 24 hours to meet with Lee at the Dabb house near Richmond in late June 1862.

Jackson had met President Davis at First Manassas. Now in the midst of the Seven Days' campaign he met him again. This time, the meeting was at the Poindexter house after the battle of Malvern Hill. McGuire had gone into a room to speak with Jackson who was with Lee and Longstreet.

Dr. McGuire relates the story of the meeting between Jackson and President Davis.

> When President Davis entered the room I recognized him and told General Jackson who he was. General Jackson believed that during the campaign through Bath and Romney with General Loring, President Davis had treated him badly... There were many other things which caused Jackson to feel rather resentful towards Mr. Davis, so when I told him who the visitor was he stood bolt upright like a corporal on guard looking at Mr. Davis. Not a muscle in his body moved. General Lee, seeing that Mr. Davis didn't know General Jackson, said: 'Why, President, don't you know Stonewall Jackson?' Mr. Davis started to greet him, evidently as warmly as those he had just left, but the appearance of Jackson stopped him, and when he

got about a yard Mr. Davis halted and Jackson immediately brought his hand up to the side of his head in military salute. Mr. Davis bowed and went back to the company in the other room.[3]

McGuire's problems, in addition to caring for the wounded, involved fighting swamp fever and malaria. The swamps and mosquitoes of the Chickahominy River made life miserable for all the troops. And Jackson's men, weakened by two months of forceful marches, lack of rest, and improper diet suffered badly. Some, including McGuire's friend Sandie Pendleton,[4] had to be sent home for rest and recuperation.

On July 13, Jackson rode from his camp south of Richmond into the city. He went to see the president and the mother of one of his men. Then the general went to the Second Presbyterian Church accompanied by Dr. McGuire. The minister was Dr. Moses D. Hoge.[5] Later, he and McGuire became very close friends and took several trips to Europe.

But on this Sunday, Jackson fell asleep in the pew. After the service, the congregation crowded around him, anxious to touch him and to talk with him. The general was embarrassed, and turning to his doctor said, "Doctor, didn't you say the horses were ready?" With that Jackson bolted from the church.[6]

A month later, Mrs. Jackson, very much concerned about the workload and the pace her husband was setting, wrote to McGuire asking him to keep a close eye on the general, and if possible, get him to slow down.[7]

Jackson apparently often fell asleep in the saddle. McGuire in an interview with a Richmond reporter states that "Many a night I have kept him (Jackson) on his horse by holding onto his coattail. He always promised to do as much for me when he had finished his nap."[8]

By August, the Union army had a new commander. Major General John Pope, who bragged that his headquarters was in the saddle, replaced McClellan. However, he had not faced Lee and Jackson.

One of McGuire's tasks was to relay casualty figures to Jackson. Jackson always wanted a detailed report, and if McGuire was detained, Jackson gave orders that he should be told the minute McGuire arrived.

The last days of August 1862 brought fighting at Groveton and Second Manassas. The Stonewall Brigade suffered heavy losses. Among the fallen was Captain Hugh White, the son of Jackson's pastor. McGuire had to tell the general that Willie Preston,[9] the son of one of the founders of the Virginia Military Institute and a close friend of Jackson's, was mortally wounded. At the news, the muscles in Jackson's face twitched, his eyes glowed. Jackson gripped McGuire's shoulder so hard that it hurt. In anger, he asked the doctor why he had left the boy. Then, Jackson walked into the woods to be alone.

McGuire continues:

> The night I told him of the number of killed—intimate personal friends of ours—of Baylor, and Neff, and Botts, and I added presently: 'We have only won this day by hard fighting.' He was full of emotion

when he turned around to me and said: 'No, sir, we have won this day by the blessing of Almighty God.'[10]

Among the wounded at Second Manassas was General Richard S. Ewell, one of Jackson's lieutenants. He was moved to a field hospital at Buckner's near Aldie. There, Dr. McGuire and Dr. S. B. Morrison operated.

Ewell's case is one of the few from the South to be included in *The Medical and Surgical History of the War of the Rebellion*. In this volume, "Wounds of the extremities were grouped according to anatomical site and the time and type of operation." Ewell's wound is recorded as one case in the 1,194 examples of primary amputation in the lower third of the femur for shot fracture.[11]

General Ewell was a poor surgical risk. He suffered from malaria and seems to have had a peptic ulcer.

Dr. McGuire writes about this case, number 447. He tells how the wound occurred, and the treatment.

> Case 447—Major-General R. S. Ewell, while commanding a division of General Jackson's Corps of the Confederate Army, was wounded in the left knee during the night of the engagement of Manassas, August 28, 1862. Dr. Hunter McGuire, Surgeon and Medical Director of the Corps, who amputated the wounded limb, published an account of the case as follows: "He was kneeling on the ground and looking under some pine bushes to get a better view of the field, when he was hit upon the left patella, nearly in the center of it, and his leg being flexed, the ball passed downward, striking the head of the tibia and splitting it into several fragments. The bullet finally lodged in the muscles of the calf of the leg. He sent for me at once, but the messenger failed to find me, and I did not know he was hurt until General Jackson sent his aide-de-camp to tell me. He was still laboring under the severe shock of the injury when I found him, although several hours had elapsed. In all gunshot wounds of the knee the shock of injury is severe, but it was especially great in this instance. The General's health, naturally not very good, was unusually bad at this time. He had also lost a great deal of sleep, and the night he was hurt was compelled to drink a large quantity of strong tea to keep awake. He was so much exhausted when he was shot that his surgeons thought at one time he would die from the shock of the injury. When he had sufficiently recovered from this, I advised him to submit to amputation; but he consented to it very reluctantly, partly because some surgeon had assured him that his wound was not dangerous, but one from which he would soon recover. I amputated the thigh just above the knee, performing the operation as rapidly and with as little loss of blood as I could. About ten days after the amputation, to escape capture, he was carried on a litter by some soldiers near fifty miles. The motion on the litter caused the bone to protrude, and in consequence of this and his bad health, the wound sloughed. After much suffering and the loss of an inch of bone, he got well enough to go about,

when one day he was so unlucky as to let his crutches slip from under him, and falling upon an icy pavement, he reopened the wound and knocked off another piece of bone.[12]

Considering the Civil War era, Ewell did rather well. He took time to recover at the home of a cousin, Dr. Jesse Ewell, in the shadow of the Bull Run Mountain, and then went to Richmond. By March of 1863, the stump was nearly healed. Several months later he was back in the saddle and riding on the roads to Gettysburg.

Dr. McGuire states, though, that "from the shape of his stump, and an ill-contrived wooded leg he wore, he was frequently troubled with abrasions of the skin small abscess, etc."[13]

On September 1, Jackson's command clashed with Union forces at Chantilly. There was a heavy downpour, with vivid flashes of lightning. It seemed that the "voice of the artillery of heaven could scarcely be told from that of the army." In the midst of the storm a courier came to Jackson from General A. P. Hill. McGuire remembers Hill saying that his ammunition was wet, and he sought to retire from the field. Jackson had another thought. "Give my compliments to General Hill, and tell him that the Yankee ammunition is just as wet as his."

# Sharpsburg and Bunker Hill

After Second Manassas, Lee wasted no time. The hour had come for him to cross the Potomac and carry the war northward—politicians in the North were saying that the war was a failure, and in September of 1862 it seemed that way. Perhaps if Lee struck quickly and hard, striking the North a Napoleonic blow, he could achieve peace. Destiny beckoned across the Potomac.

An invasion would draw Union forces from the war-torn field of Virginia. A victory in Maryland would raise Southern morale, and lower that of the North. A successful invasion might foreshadow Southern independence, especially if foreign powers recognized the Confederacy. The victory across the Potomac might cause the North to negotiate peace.[1]

Influenced by these considerations, Lee put the Army of Northern Virginia in motion. On September 4 and 5 the citizens of Leesburg, Virginia, turned out to greet the advancing Confederate columns. It was like a carnival in the streets of the town. Lee, Jackson, Longstreet, and Stuart conferred at the Harrison house on North King Street.[2] They planned the final phases of the invasion. On September 5, the infantry headed northward to the Potomac River. Most of the men were happy. Others believed they had signed up to defend their homes; they were not sure about an invasion. But the reception in Leesburg brought delight to all the men. Randolph Shotwell of the Eighth Virginia says the entire community turned out as a reception committee. Some watched quietly and anxiously for a glimpse of a son, brother, husband, or sweetheart. Occasionally, there was a scream and tears as folks learned of loved ones falling at Second Manassas. When camp was made, some local soldiers, realizing that death might be ahead in the next campaign, slipped home to be "with Polly and the babies."[3]

Jed Hotchkiss, McGuire's friend, and Jackson's map maker, describes the crossing of the Potomac:

> We started about sunrise and went, by a private road to White's Ford and there crossed the Potomac into Maryland...The 10th Virginia Regt. of

infantry, preceded by a band, and bearing a Virginia flag, was in the advance; as the band reached the Maryland shore it struck up the air, 'Maryland, My Maryland,' amid the shouts of the soldiers. It was a noble spectacle, the broad river, fringed by the lofty trees in full foliage; the exuberant wealth of the autumn wildflowers down the margin of the stream, and a bright green island stretched away to the right...We went to a lock in the canal and there intercepted a boat load of melon on the way to the Washington market, which our men bought.[4]

Heros Von Borcke, Jeb Stuart's chief of staff, describes the excitement.

> Every regiment was preparing for the march, officers were riding to and fro, and the long artillery trains were moving off along the turnpike, their rumbling noise combining with the rattle of the drums and the roll of the bugles to wake the echoes for miles around...Many a youthful hero looked forward to his triumphant entry into the Federal capital....[5]

The Tenth Virginia led one column approaching the Potomac. The flags were flying, and the band blaring the strains of "Maryland, My Maryland." Cheers swept through the ranks. The men were elated. They had reached the Potomac, another step perhaps toward victory. Many removed their shoes and rolled up their trousers. The crossing was a great spectacle.

With so many men, wagons, and equipment descending the banks of the Potomac, a huge traffic jam developed. General Jackson ordered Major John Harman to the river to unsnarl the mess. Harman was a good choice, he had operated a stagecoach line prior to the war. He was a profane man and had been rebuked by Jackson earlier. However, by choice words, skill, and threats he got the job done. Reporting to Jackson after traffic was moving smoothly, Harman said, "There's only one language that will make mules understand on a hot day."[6]

Dr. McGuire had to treat Jackson soon after entering Maryland. A person, sympathetic to the South, gave Jackson a horse. When the general sought to ride it, the horse reared and gave Jackson a nasty fall. As a result, Stonewall was unable to handle his horse for a few days and rode in an ambulance.[7]

On Saturday, September 6, Jackson's command went into camp just south of Frederick. The location was known as Best's Grove.[8] General Lee's tent was nearby. Jackson's staff and main body remained here until the morning of September 10.

It was uncertain whether or not McGuire was familiar with Frederick. His friend Sandie Pendleton knew the city because he had spent his early childhood in the Episcopal manse while his father, William Nelson Pendleton, served as the minister of All Saints Church.[9] Dr. Pendleton spent September 8 visiting former parishioners.

Young James Power Smith rode into Frederick on Sunday afternoon. He went to visit the Presbyterian Church where his father served as pastor when James was a lad. While he looked over the church, thinking about the spot where he had slept on his mother's lap, someone stole his horse, which had been tied outside.[10]

When Smith returned to camp, he was told that General Jackson wanted to see him. He thought his friends were playing a trick on him, but they were serious. Jackson wanted him to become a member of his staff. In a few months, McGuire and Smith became good friends.

Sunday evening, Jackson rode into Frederick and attended services at the German Reformed Church. He soon fell asleep, and his cap dropped to the floor. The minister prayed for President Lincoln, but Jackson didn't hear the prayer.[11]

One Monday, Jackson wrote to his wife lamenting that he had fallen asleep. He was impressed with Frederick, saying, "The town appears to be a charming place." It reminded him of Lexington.[12]

One of the purposes of the Maryland campaign was to gain recruits for the Confederate cause. Maryland was a border state and hopefully it could be induced to unite with the Confederacy. On the eighth, Lee issued a proclamation to the people of Maryland, urging their support, saying it was natural they should side with the South. However, he said Maryland would be welcome "only if you come of your own will."

Maryland listened and observed and did not respond. This may have been due to the condition of Lee's troops. They were well behaved and respectful, but most were shoeless, many were hatless, while their uniforms were dirty and almost threadbare. Some of the residents were amazed that such a ragtag army could be so successful. One lady thought the scarecrows in her fields were better dressed than the Confederate soldiers.[13]

Lee had expected his advance into Maryland to cause the evacuation of Union forces from Harpers Ferry, thereby opening his lines to supply and to communication with the Shenandoah Valley. This did not occur. So, Lee had to divide his army to achieve this purpose. Special Order No. 191 was written giving directions to each command to regroup at Boonsboro or Hagerstown in Washington County, Maryland.

"At an early hour," Jackson's preferred time, the general and his men left Frederick. Their objective was to capture Martinsburg and Harpers Ferry, securing Lee's flank and lines of communication. Federal patrols almost captured Henry Douglas and Jackson[14] on the western slopes of South Mountain near Boonsboro. Eluding the patrols, they crossed the Potomac and entered Martinsburg.

On Sunday, September 14, while part of Lee's army was fighting to hold back the advance of the Union army under General George B. McClellan at Fox's, Turner's and Crampton's Gaps in the South Mountain range, Jackson closed in on Harpers Ferry. Elements of the Confederate army under Major General Lafayette McLaws and Brigadier General John G. Walker gained possession of Maryland and Loudoun Heights. As guns were trained on Harpers Ferry, the town was doomed.

On Monday morning, Confederate artillery opened fire from the mountain heights in Virginia and Maryland. General A. P. Hill's infantry of Jackson's command advanced upon the town. Soon, a white flag of surrender was seen flying from the Union position. Over 11,000 men and vast stores of supplies were captured by Jackson. By the middle of the morning, Jackson was able to send a courier to Lee

# Sharpsburg and Bunker Hill

with the message, "Through God's blessing, Harpers Ferry and its garrison are to be surrendered."[15] Hill was left to take care of the surrender, while Jackson and the rest of the command started for Sharpsburg.

About daybreak on the fifteenth, Lee's ragged, footsore veterans took up position on the west bank of the Antietam Creek, between the stream and the little German farming village of Sharpsburg. Lee's line of defense was a fairly good one, three miles long with its left flank on the Potomac, and the right on the west bank of the Antietam, opposite the lower or Rohrback Bridge. Lee was on a hill just outside the town when he received news of the fall of Harpers Ferry. "This is good news," he said, "let it be announced to the troops."[16] Jackson's men spent the rest of the day tramping toward the Potomac and reunion with Lee at Sharpsburg.

September 16 was a day of unrest and anxiety in the Valley of the Antietam. The fields were full of soldiers, wagons, and cannons.

> The operations which resulted in the capture of Harpers Ferry had been arduous in the extreme. Men who had taken part in the forced marches in the Valley campaign declared that the march from Frederick to Harpers Ferry surpassed all former experiences. In three and a half days they had covered over sixty miles...The weather had been intensely hot, and the dust was terrible. This night march, coming on top of their previous exertions, had taxed the strength of many beyond endurance.[17]

Once again, McGuire had to treat men for sore feet and fatigue.

Jackson's command crossed the Potomac south of Ferry Hill, the home of Henry Douglas, at Boteler's, or Pack Horse Ford. Part of the command stacked arms in a field about a mile from Sharpsburg, while the rest continued to a position near a little white, brick German Baptist Church, north of Sharpsburg.

McClellan's plan of battle was to strike the left flank of the Confederate army, then the right, and when both assaults were going well, launch a major strike at the center of Lee's line.

At dawn, the Union artillery opened fire on the Confederate positions. From the cover of the Poffenberger farm and the North Woods, still veiled by morning mists, the Union attack column moved forward. General Joseph Hooker was advancing with three infantry divisions against Stonewall Jackson. The objective was the high grounds around the little Dunkard Church.

The fighting was severe. Soldiers fell as though they had been cut down with a scythe. General Hooker reported, "It was never my fortune to witness a more bloody, dismal battlefield." Jackson's forces met the Union troops "with the utmost resolution...and the conflict raged with great fury and alternate success." Losses reached 50 percent in most of Jackson's command. Major General John B. Hood's men came to Jackson's support. They drove the men in blue back, but suffered heavy losses. In two hours of bitter fighting approximately 12,000 Union infantry engaged 10,000 Confederates. The losses were staggering. Jackson lost 2,438 men, and McGuire had 1,859 wounded to treat.

Jackson established headquarters at the David Smith farm at the west end of Sharpsburg on the road to Shepherdstown.[18] McGuire also established his hospital on this farm. Throughout the day, there was a steady stream of ambulances and litter bearers coming to the farm.

Losses had mounted so quickly during the morning that McGuire rode to see Jackson near the front and asked him about the possibility of moving the wounded to Shepherdstown.

Jackson, seated in the saddle on Little Sorrel, gladly accepted the peaches McGuire offered him. While the doctor and the general were talking, Jackson pointed in the direction of the enemy and said to McGuire, "They have done their worst."[19]

When things quieted down around the Dunkard Church, the action shifted to a sunken road, which soon would be called "Bloody Lane." In the afternoon, the third in the series of Union attacks was launched at the stone bridge south of Sharpsburg.

Union forces finally crossed "Burnside Bridge" and were driving the Confederates back toward the Harpers Ferry Road. "Lee was enduring his most anxious moments of the war.[20] His army was in great danger. Just in time, the troops of General A. P. Hill reached the field. They had completed a 17-mile march, forded the Potomac, and now they struck the flank of Burnside's Corps with vengeance. Hill, picturesque in his red battle shirt, was all over the field giving directions. He had arrived "not a moment too soon."[21] Such a day of suspense and danger, Lee had never known.

> Across the din of battle could be heard the...wild rebel yell. Red banners were following stars and stripes. Ragged boys in butternut leaped over prone bodies in blue. The roar of the guns on the heights swelled to a pitch of triumph yard by yard as the Union line, sagging and gapping but unbroken, fell back to the shelter of the low ridges near the creek.[22]

The bloody battle of Antietam came to an end, just as the setting sun, a crimson red, sank beyond the western hills. General James Longstreet, one of Lee's corps commanders, wrote:

> For fourteen long hours more than one hundred thousand men with five hundred pieces of artillery had engaged in titanic combat. As the pall of battle smoke rose and cleared away, the scene presented was to make the stoutest heart shudder. There lay upon the ground, scattered for three miles over the valleys and the hills or in improvised hospitals, more than twenty thousand men....[23]

In three distinct areas, the battle had raged. For McClellan, the story in each action was "almost, but not quite successful"; for the Confederates, "we held on." Each action had taken a heavy toll. As the sounds of battle died away, the cannon could cool, and men could collect their wits.

However, there would be no rest this September night for Dr. McGuire or any of the other army doctors. Colonel Francis Palfrey gave this graphic description of the terrible night.

> The blessed night came, and brought with it sleep and forgetfulness and refreshment to many; but the murmur of the night wind, breathing

over the fields of wheat and clover, was mingled with the groans of the countless suffered of both armies. Who can tell, who can imagine, the horrors of such a night....[24]

Colonel R. L. Walker, a Confederate officer, writes:

...all night long their lanterns (those of the ambulance corps) could be seen flashing about the battlefield while they were searching for friend and foe alike....[25]

General Lee held a council of war at the Grove house on the square in Sharpsburg. He asked each officer about the condition of their troops and the losses they had incurred. Turning to John B. Hood, Lee asked, "How's your fine division?" Hood had a short answer, "Dead upon the field, sir."[26]

After the Seven Days' campaign, McClellan had assigned Jonathan Letterman as his medical director. Letterman did an amazing job in reorganizing the medical situation, setting up unit hospitals and designating litter bearers from each regiment. Antietam was the first time he was able to put his plans into operation. Prior to this battle, some of the wounded lay upon the field for several days. However, even those wounded while falling back to Burnside Bridge were rescued before morning. These efforts undoubtedly saved many lives. Principles of Letterman's plan still exist in the U.S. Army Medical Corps. McGuire had the same plan in operation during the Valley campaign and used it at Sharpsburg.

The two armies regrouped on September 18, caring for the wounded, burying the dead and dying, and collecting weapons from the field.

Dr. McGuire was extremely busy deciding which patients to take across the river and which ones were too badly wounded to move. He supervised the loading of the horse-drawn vehicles that took the wounded to the Potomac River and across to Shepherdstown.

The town that seemed like it had been forgotten in the great bend of the Potomac[27] was ready to experience the trauma of war. On Monday, many of the wounded from Boonsboro had been brought to Shepherdstown. Hospitals were set up in churches, large halls, and in vacant rooms. Children brought bundles of hay and straw for the floor. Blankets were obtained from private homes. These were placed on top of the straw. "On these improvised beds the suffering men were placed, the next question was how to properly dress their wounds. No surgeons were to be seen...."[28] Mary Bedinger Mitchell and the other ladies in Shepherdstown...

set bravely to work, and washed away the blood or staunched it as well as they could. (The wounds had reopened as a result of the jolting ride)...Then there was the hunt for bandages. Every housekeeper ransacked her stores and brought forth things new and old. I saw one girl...look about helplessly, and then rip off the hem of her white petticoat....[29]

The doctors came and performed rough surgery. The women, untrained though they were, assisted, handing the doctors their instruments, holding the basins, and trying to soothe the wounded. The emergency brought forth the best in the women.

One young lady worked on the sidewalk, and then in a small, hot room. She said:

> The sights and smells so overcame me that I staggered to the staircase, where I flung myself over the bannister, saying to myself, "Oh, I hope if I faint some one will kick me into the corner and let me lie there."[30]

She did not faint, but went back to work in a few moments and served the rest of the day. Even the children helped to alleviate the suffering of the Confederate wounded. The sights and sounds experienced by the women of Shepherdstown on these September days were part of the daily life of Dr. McGuire.

Mrs. Mitchell continues her dramatic story.

> On the 17th cloudy skies looked down upon the two armies facing each other in the fields of Maryland. It seems to me that the roar of the day began with the light and all through its long and dragging hours its thunder formed a background to our pain and terror. We went about our work, nursing the Confederate wounded from South Mountain with pale faces and trembling hands, yet trying to appear composed for the sake of our patients, who were much excited.
>
> We could hear the incessant explosions of artillery, the shrieking whistles of the shells, and the sharper rolls of musketry.
>
> On our side of the Potomac there was noise, confusion, dust; throngs of stragglers, horsemen galloping about; wagons blocking each other, and teamsters wangling; and a continued din of shouting, swearing, and rumbling. In the midst of all of this men were dying. Fresh loads of wounded were constantly arriving. The surgeons were busy amputating limbs and dressing wounds. The women of Shepherdstown did their best to assist, bringing bandages, medicine, and food to the Confederate doctors.
>
> That night was dark and the air heavy and dull. Across the river innumerable campfires were blazing. We could well imagine the dreadful scenes they were lighting. We sat in silence, looking only into each other's tired faces. There were no impatient words, few tears; only silence, and a drawing close together, as if for comfort. We could not believe that anything human could have escaped from the appalling fire.
>
> On Thursday the two armies lay idly facing each other, but we could not be idle. The Confederate wounded continued to arrive until the town was quite unable to hold all the disabled and suffering. They filled every building and overflowed into the country around, into farmhouses, barns, corncribs, cabins—wherever four walls and a roof were found together. Those able to travel were sent to Winchester and towns back from the river. But their departure seemed to make no appreciable difference. There are six churches in Shepherdstown. They are all filled with wounded. The Odd Fellows' Hall, the Freemasons, the little Town Council room, the barnlike place known as the Drill Room, all private homes, the shops, and empty buildings, the schoolhouses, every inch of space, filled with wounded from Antietam. Yet more space was needed.

Even the unfinished Town Hall was placed into service. Rough boards were thrown across the beams, piles of straw on top, and we had another hospital. As a last resort, the old stone warehouses down by the river were thrown open. They were very musty and dirty after years of being closed. But they were aired out, swept, and convened into hospital use.[31]

Some of these poor lads, aided by the women of Shepherdstown, were those brought to town by Dr. McGuire. The area was "one vast hospital."[32] Union reports show that 309 of the Confederates who were left behind and taken prisoner died. Among them who were 19 at McGuire's main hospital on the David Smith farm.[33]

During the night of the eighteenth, the Confederate army crossed the Potomac into what is now Jefferson County, West Virginia. General Lee sat on his horse in the middle of the river. When told the last wagon was approaching, he said, "Thank God."[34]

Dr. Letterman reports there were 27 hospitals of considerable size caring for the Union wounded. In Frederick, where many were sent along with the wounded Confederates found on the field, there were 62 surgeons, 539 nurses, and 127 cooks[35] working in the hospitals.

After Sharpsburg, the Confederate army reorganized in camps near Winchester, Berryville, and Bunker Hill. October was hot and dry. Living and working together in the military, a very close friendship developed between Hunter McGuire, Henry Douglas, and Sandie Pendleton. They had much in common. They were all college graduates. They came from prominent families. They had hopes for the future, and they shared common views on states' rights and their allegiance to Virginia.

Sandie wrote home describing their living quarters. He used Douglas's haversack as his desk, while sitting on a camp stool in front of a stove captured from the Yankees. Douglas slept on one side of the tent. His bed consisted of a pile of blankets. McGuire and Pendleton shared a bed together, such as it was. On one side of the tent was their trunks. Clothing hung from a suspended rod. And in order of appearance, this was the list on October 26: "Dr. McGuire's spurs, my holster with a pair of loaded revolvers, Henry Douglas's ditto, Dr. McGuire's towel, his holster and pistols, my sword belt, a new and handsome sword captured at Harpers Ferry, my spurs...Douglas's sword and belt, his towel, Dr. McGuire's canteen and overcoat." Rubber raincoats, pipes, tobacco, a copy of Shakespeare, Sandie's prayer book, and a pile of firewood completed the furnishings.[36]

The three friends liked to read. They shared the contents of their books with each other. Shakespeare was a favorite, and apparently McGuire was the best reader. Mid-October brought a shortage of rations to headquarters. For 10 days brave soldiers lived on bread and beef. Sugar and coffee supplies were also exhausted.

The weather turned cold on October 24. Dr. McGuire came to Jackson's aid. The general writes: "But my good friend Dr. Hunter McGuire secured a camp stove for me...and I am (quite comfortable today)."[37]

A week later, McGuire and his friends feasted on a Sunday dinner complete with boiled turkey, bacon, cabbage, and all sorts of vegetables. The fortunes of war had shifted and there was good food again.

# Chapter 11

During the bivouac in the Bunker Hill area, Jackson took one day, the only day during the war, for a social event. He rode with Dr. McGuire to Winchester to make some social calls. The general took dinner with Dr. and Mrs. Hugh McGuire, Hunter's parents. Dr. Graham was also present. While they were eating, Betty McGuire, Hunter's sister, asked Jackson for a picture. He said he had none to give. Betty replied, "Well then, why don't you have one taken." Accordingly, Jackson went to a nearby photographer's shop. Just before the picture was to be taken, Mr. Routzhan noticed a button was missing from Jackson's coat. Taking the button from his pocket, Jackson asked for a needle and thread and sewed the button back on. The button, a little bit out of line, can still be seen in the picture, third button from the top, on the left.[38] [See photograph on p. 46.]

Many local citizens had lost loved ones due to combat, sickness, or disease. Cornelia McDonald was saddened by the death of her daughter. She expressed her own sentiments as well as those of many others in these words:

> The low moon is shining brightly, casting big black shadows on the ground. The whippoorwill has come again, and is making the night sadder with his melancholy call. I sit at the window late, when everybody else is asleep, to think of the past, and try to live over again the pleasant days that are gone...
>
> The autumn winds are whirling away the leaves from the trees, the sunshine looks cold and sad...Since last autumn what a harvest Death has reaped! Where is the home that is not shadowed by grief, or the heart that has not received a blow...?[39]

John Garibaldi, a member of the Stonewall Brigade, says that the weeks are pleasant and peaceful. But camp life and inactivity soon brought boredom.[40] It was drill, picket duty, police the area, the same routine every day. Those who could slipped away from camp and went into Winchester or other nearby villages.

At the beginning of the autumn, Jeb Stuart's cavalry was camped several miles away at the Bower. Occasionally, the staffs of the two officers visited the encampments of the other.

With a lull in the fighting, and camp set up in the same spot for several days, religious services were begun on a nightly basis. A great revival was soon in progress with many conversions. At least 35 men in the Stonewall Brigade made professions of faith. Jackson was happy about this because he wanted a godly army.

One night Jackson and Douglas walked through the bivouac area of the Stonewall Brigade. The men were sitting around in groups of four, many of them playing cards. Candles stuck in inverted bayonets provided light. As the general approached, cards were put away, lights were extinguished, and the men followed their commander to church under the stars. They listened to their preacher and to General Jackson pray for them and for peace. McGuire attended some of these services because he appears in the drawing of the journalist who was present one night. When the service was over, the men walked back to their tents. The stars were shining brightly and there was a full moon. As the drums beat tattoo, the troops let loose with the famous Rebel yell. To Jackson, and perhaps to McGuire, it was "the sweetest music I ever heard."[41]

Many individuals sought interviews with the former professor who was now a world renown military leader. Among those coming to headquarters at Bunker Hill was Lieutenant Colonel Garnet Wolseley. He had been sent as an observer by the queen of England. In time he became a very good friend of McGuire, and still later, commander in chief of the British army.

Dr. Hugh McGuire showed his stubborn streak as he defied his wife and son Hunter by wanting to go to Lexington. Mrs. McGuire, knowing that her husband was not well and realizing that the Union troops could retake Winchester at any time, asked Hunter to use his office to keep his father at home.

Although difficult for Hunter to do, he wrote an order directing his father to stay in Winchester to care for the wounded. The message was delivered by courier. It was addressed:

To: Surgeon Hugh Holmes McGuire<br>
From: Medical Director of Army<br>
Subject: Assignment to Duty

Ten miles out of Winchester, Hunter was overtaken by his father mounted on his favorite horse. The horse was laden with saddle bags packed to the hilt. Dr. Hugh McGuire passed his son without a nod.

Hunter called to the courier and asked if he had delivered the message. The courier replied, "Yes."

"Well, what did he say?" inquired Hunter.

The embarrassed courier said, "Tell Hunter he is a damned fool."

The elderly Hugh was not about to listen to Mrs. McGuire or to Hunter. He was on his way to Lexington to take care of the wounded in the hospital there.[42]

It was about time for the rest of the army to leave too. Lincoln had replaced General George B. McClellan with General Ambrose P. Burnside. The Union army was at Warrenton ready to move on Fredericksburg and perhaps Richmond.

# XII

# Fredericksburg and Moss Neck

Late in November, Jackson and his staff headed south from Winchester. McGuire, Pendleton, and Hotchkiss were near the general. As they traveled the Valley Pike, they stopped to look at the battlefield at Kernstown. Reaching New Market, the column turned to look back over the Shenandoah Valley. For Jackson and one-fourth of the command, this would be their final look. As they climbed the mountain, there was elation. Jackson's men were anxious to meet the men in blue. The battle at Sharpsburg had not dampened their feelings of confidence. "They'd 'whup' them this time." One more victory might get them home in time to do the spring plowing. Sandie Pendleton wrote: "Our corps musters thirty thousand men for duty...in as fine trim and eager for another fight as I have seen during the war."[1]

The families in the Shenandoah watched in sorrow and dread as their husbands, sons, and brothers went off to fight again. Many wives and mothers already wore black, mourning for loved ones. As night came, the moon cast shadows, and the whippoorwills gave forth their haunting calls.[2]

There was snow in Winchester on December 4. It looked so lovely from Cornelia McDonald's farmhouse window. The cedar trees were covered. The green branches looked like they were covered with white sheaths. Everything was so clear and distinct in the moonlight. But Mrs. McDonald was thinking of her husband and others away at war, sleeping on the ground, often without the shelter of even tents. Happy times seemed so far away. No longer was there the tingle of sleighbells, and the laughter of voices playing in the snow. "All is past now, and gone, I feel, forever...I cannot feel happier when I see and know of so much misery. Scarcely a household that I know but has a vacant place, and a fireside but where there are breaking hearts and wants."[3]

This was Hunter McGuire's Winchester in December of 1862. Making matters worse, Union troops occupied Winchester once again, this time men under the command of General James Geary. Jackson and his corps were on the verge of another big battle. This time at Fredericksburg, on the banks of the Rappahannock River.

# Fredericksburg and Moss Neck

The weather was now clear and cold. There was a lack of good clothing and overcoats. Some of the troops were still without shoes. But men under Jackson plodded on through Orange County, Gordonsville, Chancellorsville, and then on December 2, made camp at Guiney's Station, 10 miles south of Fredericksburg along the Richmond, Fredericksburg, and Potomac Railroad. General Burnside and the Union army were on the move. Generals Lee and Jackson had to get between the Union commander and Richmond.

In preparation for his assault and as a cover for the laying of his pontoon bridges, Burnside ordered cannons to open fire on Fredericksburg. The effect was devastating. An estimated 15,000 shells fell on the town. Gaping holes were seen in most buildings. Clouds of fire, dust, and smoke filled the air.

As the fog lifted on December 13, Burnside sent column after column against the troops of Jackson and Longstreet, entrenched on a line from Marye's Heights to Hamilton's Crossing. Lee had had time to train 275 guns on the field of the Union advance. The Confederacy had approximately 80,000 men in place to defend against the Union attack.

About 10 A.M. the brilliant rays of the December sun dispelled the morning mists. The Confederates saw an amazing display. In front of them were massed columns of union infantry. Officers dashed up and down the lines giving orders, and then they started forward. On and on they came. The Confederates waited, and then they opened a murderous fire. Gaps were torn in the Union lines by the volleys of shot and shell. Union troops went down as thickly as Jackson's men had gone down in the Miller cornfield at Sharpsburg. The men in blue were brave as they did their best, but no one could stand against the withering fire of the Confederate infantry and artillery. It was a colossal blunder on the part of General Burnside. He proved, as he said, that he was unfit to lead the army. And the cost was thousands of young men.

Burnside seemed unwilling to admit failure, or that his plans were futile. He ordered wave after wave of troops forward in suicidal charges. Maybe he thought the Confederates would run out of ammunition, or that constant hammering would break the Rebel line.

Jed Hotchkiss described the action.

> Saturday, December 13th. We were up at an early hour and off to the battlefield by daylight. The morning was cool but the sun rose red and fiery and soon drove away the fog....The Federal infantry advanced about 1:30 p.m. and incessant firing was kept up at intervals during the rest of the day....Our position was a very fine one, our men sheltered by the woods, but we had many killed and wounded by the shells of the enemy from long-range guns.[4]

The night of December 13 was bitterly cold. Thousands of Union lay wounded beside their dead comrades in front of Jackson's lines. They were in pain and freezing from the severe weather. Many died that night from their wounds and exposure.

Things were better for the Confederates. They had fought a defensive battle, and their hospitals were in secure positions behind their lines. Jackson's staff was intact, although Pendleton had been bruised by a Minié ball. It cut through both coats and hit a knife in his trouser's pocket. He was not hurt otherwise.[5]

That night from the Confederate lines, the haunting refrains of "Annie Laurie" drifted over the battlefield. And the northern lights filled the night sky with an amazing display of colors.[6]

Dr. McGuire gave Jackson a preliminary report of the casualties including General Maxcy Gregg of South Carolina. McGuire gives an account of the event.

> I told General Jackson, as I usually did, as far as I knew, of friends and prominent men killed and wounded. I had gotten to headquarters right late and found the General awake. Among others I mentioned General Gregg's case. He said: "I wish you would go back and see him. Tell him I want you to see him." I demurred a little, saying it had not been very long since I had seen him; that he was mortally wounded and that there was nothing to be done for him. He said: "I wish you would go and see him; tell him I sent you." So I mounted my horse and rode to the Yerby house and saw General Gregg, who was slowly getting worse, and delivered the message. I had hardly gotten out of the room into the hall when I met General Jackson, who must have ridden very close behind me to have reached there so soon. He stopped me, asked about General Gregg, and went into the room to see him. No one else was in the room. What passed between these two officers no one will ever know. I waited for him and rode back to camp with him. He did not speak a word on the way. When we got to the camp he looked up at the sky for a moment and said: "How horrible is war!" I said: "Horrible, yes; but we have been invaded. What can we do?" "Do!" he said, and his manner was savage and his voice ringing. "Do? Thrash them!" If he had lived we would have done it.[7]

On December 16 the Union forces recrossed the Rappahannock River during the previous night. Then a report reached Confederate headquarters that Union forces were crossing at Port Royal to the south side of the river. Jackson put his troops in motion to check this potential threat. When they reached the vicinity of Moss Neck, word came from General Jeb Stuart that it was just a rumor. So a halt was made in a thicket of pines.

Jackson and the staff had been in the front. Now, they sought to get to the rear. To do so, they had to ride single file through the columns of infantry. "The men were in fine spirits and kept cheering for the entire staff and escort that followed the general."[8] Hotchkiss' notes continue the story:

> After getting through the thicket-enclosed road we turned to the right and rode down through open woods to a sheltered hollow and went into bivouac where the fallen leaves were abundant. Someone started a fire at the base of a large, hollow tulip poplar, the ascending sparks of which afforded a subject for conversation between the general and the staff. We tried to induce the general to go into a house, as the air was sharp and raw, and we had nothing to eat. But he refused, and we soon laid down in a circle around the roaring fire with our feet toward it. About 10 p.m. the tree

burned off and fell with a crash, but fortunately did not hit anyone. By that time we were all well chilled and when we renewed our request to go to a house he yielded and Pendleton and I rode forward in search of Corbin's place, and having found it easily secured an invitation to come to "Moss Neck," the palatial home of Corbin, and Hd. Qrs. were established there late in the night. The troops bivouacked near where they were halted.[9]

Seven generations of Corbins had made their home at Moss Neck in the Rappahannock River Valley. They had married the Lees, the Byrds, the Carters, and others belonging to the first families of Virginia. Richard Corbin, the current owner, was away at war with the Ninth Virginia Cavalry. Now Roberta (Bertie) and her sister-in-law Kate were trying to operate the plantation.

Several days earlier, Bertie and Kate had ridden across the fields to watch the Union assault on Fredericksburg.[10] Being Virginians and sympathetic to the war effort, they were happy to have Jackson and his staff in their home. The staff had intended just to spend the night. When morning came though, the ladies prepared and served a fine breakfast. They invited the general to make his headquarters at Moss Neck.

Jackson was grateful for the offer, but his men had to camp outside in the winter weather. He would share their plight and refused the kind invitation. In a few days the general caught a bad cold. This time Dr. McGuire urged him to move inside. Reluctantly, Jackson relented and compromised. He did move into a small frame building, which had served as the plantation office.

Jeb Stuart and Henry Douglas teased Jackson about his new facility. The library of one of the owners of Moss Neck was in the building. He must have been a very worldly man. The books and pictures were just the opposite of Jackson's philosophy of life.[11]

Christmas was approaching, and Sandie Pendleton received an early gift. On December 23, McGuire's tent mate and friend was promoted to major and named assistant adjutant general of the Second Corps.[12]

Sandie had other interests, as did the other men on the staff. They were all impressed with Kate Corbin, the sister of the owner of Moss Neck. Kate was just 23 in 1862, young, lovely, and high spirited. Her eyes were bewitching. She was considered a "great belle."[13] Many young men sought to win her hand, and Sandie Pendleton was one of them.

Christmas Eve brought peace and quiet to the Rappahannock. Union and Confederate pickets along the river swapped newspapers, tobacco, and coffee. Then under the stars, from their positions along the river, they sang carols to one another.

Two days prior to Christmas, Jackson told Captain James P. Smith that he wanted to entertain Lee, Stuart, and Dr. Pendleton "at a dinner on Christmas day." Smith was placed in charge of the elaborate preparations. The officers of the Confederacy and the staff of the Second Corps had a banquet complete with turkey, ham, and oysters. Much of the food had been sent by admirers of Jackson. It was a Christmas dinner which those present would never forget.

After the dinner in Jackson's office, the staff went in the evening to an old-fashioned Christmas dinner in the Corbin mansion. Douglas enjoyed himself and he and Dr. McGuire played with Jane Welford Corbin, the five-year-old daughter of Richard and Bertie Corbin. In the months to come she was to bring great joy to Jackson. Little Janie

>...unconscious of her country's and parent's struggles, happy in her innocence and ignorance. I bless her for the pleasant recollection she has recalled for me and fervently hope that her future Christmases may always be as bright and free from sorrow as this one.[14]

As the evening faded away, Douglas had other thoughts of "those I laughed with one year ago and of many who laughed with me, and will laugh no more in this life. May this be the last year of this war I would earnestly pray."[15]

Douglas thought the Corbin home was "one of the finest mansions I have ever seen in Virginia." His presence with the Corbin family, surrounded by the members of the staff who were his close friends, helped him as he reflected on 1862.

Sandie Pendleton had his thoughts too. But first, he had a task to perform. Writing to his mother and relatives in Lexington, he asked them to assist Dr. Hugh McGuire, Hunter's father, now in his sixties, who was serving in the army hospital in Lexington. The elder McGuire had been so kind to him while he had been in Winchester; now, he hoped his family would return the favor.[16]

Looking back over the year, Sandie regretted being on the battlefields for eight Sundays, "hearing the roar of the battle and the groans of the dying and wounded rather than the praises of God and thanksgiving." Sandie hoped the end of 1863 would find him home, enjoying "the peace and independence which have been so well earned."[17] He writes to his mother:

>Here I am in this blustering night of the 31st of December in a tent on the banks of the Rappahannock, sitting by a blazing fire in as nice a hearth as you ever saw. It is really cheerful to sit by the fireside, and face the year going out in peace, and I accept it as a good omen that we spend the time so differently from what it was a year ago.[18]

During January, Sandie, Stapleton Crutchfield, a young artillery officer, and McGuire continued to read the works of Shakespeare, and Dickens's *A Tale of Two Cities*. Sometimes Sandie rode to inspect Confederate positions. Occasionally, Dr. McGuire rode with him. However, more often his companion was Kate Corbin. The romance was beginning to bloom.

On January 6, 1863, Jackson's staff witnessed a grand review of General A. P. Hill's division on the neighboring Hayfield estate. The parade was marred by a cold rain.[19] The next day an accounting was given of the funds that headquarters had raised for the relief of the residents of Fredericksburg. The funds amounted to a contribution of $800.

Kate Corbin wrote to her friends saying that the Virginia officers were of good stock "and hard to beat. We have a great deal of music and some of the gentlemen have fine voices; and one of the best bands in the corps is camped close to us." The music must have made an impression on Kate. She quoted some of the "Song of the Rebel":

> They will tell their children
> Though all the other memories fade
> That they fought with Stonewall Jackson
> In the old Stonewall Brigade.[20]

On February 21 she wrote to friends lamenting the possibility of Jackson's command leaving Moss Neck. "Wither shall I go? And what shall I do? We will miss our constant visitors and hate desperately to part with some of those who will have to leave us." She continues by saying that

> my particular friends are Lt. Smith and Major Pendleton of the General's staff. I wish you could see them. You could not help liking both, and I feel assured I have succeeded in making them real friends of mine.[21]

Meanwhile, the Stonewall Brigade had erected a chapel. The revival that had begun at Bunker Hill continued to progress. And for amusement, the troops engaged in snowball battles. McGuire seems to have had mostly routine camp and administrative duty. February 25, 1863, marked the anniversary of James K. Boswell's reporting to General Jackson. "I then saw my hero for the first time." After the introduction, Boswell started on his first scout duty for Jackson. Now a year later, the young officer reflects on the events of the period.

> How long it seems since that day; it appears more like ten years than one; the truth is that I have thought, felt, and acted more in the last year than in all the rest of my life. I have been present in ten hard-fought and bloody battles....I have heard the wild cry of victory as it rose above the roar of the cannon and musket. I have seen the field strewn with thousands of corpses, both of friend and foe. I have heard the groans of the wounded and dying. I have seen the fairest portions of the Old Dominion desolated by the ravages of...war. I have seen towns ransacked, and hundreds...of helpless women and children thrown homeless...I have seen, too, the bodies of our gallant men in the last agonies of death. Oh, war, why art thou called glorious when such are thy fruits? How long must our dear land be desolated by the ravages and our bravest sacrificed upon thy altars?...Oh! What changes this year have wrought in my feelings. One year ago I was full of life and animation, hope dressed the future...all my dreams of happiness were cherished as though I were sure of their realization....[22]

March 8 brought sadness and personal loss to Hunter McGuire. On this Sunday, he buried his personal servant. The two men had been like brothers. Unfortunately, we do not know the name of his friend or the cause of death. With the coming of night McGuire visited Hotchkiss to discuss his grief.[23] In the following days, General Jackson spent much time seeking to comfort the young doctor, sharing words from the Scriptures and his own deep faith. The Winchester physician was forever grateful and always remembered the general and the comfort he gave in a moment of deep, personal sorrow. In Hunter's words, "He came to my tent and spent an hour with me, comforting me in his simple, kindly, Christian way, showing a depth of friendship and affection which can never be forgotten."[24]

The death of his servant was but the beginning of the sorrows to come. Throughout the winter, Janie Corbin made deep impressions on all the men. She was very close to Hunter; Janie was also Jackson's favorite. She spent the late afternoons in his office. It was strange to see the general, who had brought fear to the North, playing with paper dolls on the floor of his office with little Janie. She had been impressed with his golden braid. The general, never one for show, gave the braid to Janie.

In mid-March, disease struck Moss Neck. Janie and her two cousins, who were spending the winter, became very ill with scarlet fever. McGuire checked them daily. He did all he could to help the children.

Spring was coming and that meant campaigning. So in the midst of his grief over his servant, and his distress over the sickness of the children, McGuire had to prepare to leave. Headquarters was to be moved to the Yerby homestead, nearer to Hamilton's Crossing and Fredericksburg.[25]

Captain James Boswell summarized the feeling of the staff:

> I fear that our memories of this camp will by no means be as pleasant as those of Moss Neck, for we certainly have been most fortunate in our winter quarters, and we shall always look back to the three months spent at Moss Neck with no small degree of pleasure. Mrs. Corbin and Miss Kate shall always have my best wishes.[26]

On March 16, Jackson and most of the staff left Moss Neck. The general's last act was to go to Janie's bedside and give her a good-bye. Sandie and Hunter remained another day at Moss Neck.

In mid-morning on the seventeenth, Pendleton went to see Janie. She seemed better. Mrs. Corbin went to take care of some household duties. Moments after Sandie stepped out of the room, Mrs. Dickinson came running and asked him to check on Janie. She was ice cold. Sandie ran to the yard and summoned Dr. McGuire.[27] There was nothing he could do. Little Janie, the darling of Moss Neck, was dead. Mrs. Corbin became hysterical. McGuire probably agreed with Sandie as he said, "Death on the battlefield is not half so fearful as this." The two young officers felt they had lived years in the moments by Janie's deathbed.

When Jackson received the news of her passing he wept and dispatched Captain James Smith to assist the family.

Janie's cousins also died. The carpenters of the Stonewall Brigade made the caskets for the little bodies. Jackson and the staff attended the service.

Sandie wrote to Kate saying that Dr. McGuire was "sorely afflicted as if it were his own; his tender heart was deeply affected by the mother's grief."[28] McGuire lamented that his best efforts were not good enough. He was powerless to curb the scarlet fever.

Pendleton and McGuire shared the same tent for the next six weeks at Hamilton's Crossing. McGuire tried to keep as busy as possible, seeking to keep his mind off the deaths of the children. Whenever duty permitted, Sandie rode back to Moss Neck to spend time with Kate. And in late April they announced their engagement. Jackson was happy and paid Sandie a rare compliment. "If he makes as good a husband as he has a soldier, Miss Corbin will do well."[29]

Mrs. Jackson arrived on April 21. She stayed with her husband at Thomas Yerby's. This was the first time the general had seen his little daughter, Julia, born in November. On April 23, McGuire and the rest of the staff gathered in the parlor at the Yerby home and rejoiced as the Reverend Beverly Lacy baptized the daughter of General and Mrs. Jackson.[30]

On April 29, came the sounds of action. The new Union commander, General Joseph Hooker, was advancing. Captain Smith broke the news to Jackson. His wife was sent to Richmond. Soon the camps were struck and the Second Corps prepared for action.[31]

In Winchester, the weather was warm and delightful. Yet "the moon looked down through bare branches. The spring seems reluctant to put on her beautiful robes where there is so much sorrow and desolation everywhere."[32]

Perhaps it was an omen of things to come for McGuire, Jackson, and the South. Miles away Lee and Jackson met at the forks of a road to plan strategy. The place was called Chancellorsville.

# XIII

## Chancellorsville

West of Fredericksburg the dim light of a small campfire casts flickering shadows on the pine trees and the road. The location was where the Orange Plank Road crosses a dirt road to Catharine Furnace.

> The night was chilly for the first of May. Two picturesque figures, seated on discarded Federal cracker boxes and silhouetted against the backdrop of trees, pulled their military greatcoats closer about their bodies in protest against the inadequate warmth from the crackling firewood.[1]

Captain James P. Smith witnessed the council:

> I had to rub my eyes and collect my wits to recognize the figures of Robert E. Lee and Stonewall Jackson. Who can tell the story of that quiet council of war between two sleeping armies?[2]

Lee and Jackson were planning something big, a flank march to attack the Union right. By five o'clock James Smith, who witnessed the candlelight council of war, was up, following Jackson's order to get the men moving.

Although outnumbered by Hooker and the Union army opposing them, Jackson would march by the old road and turn and attack Union forces camped west of Chancellorsville. Reverend Beverly Lacy and others familiar with the area led the way. It took a long time to move his command. But by quarter past five that Saturday afternoon, Jackson asked his commanders, "Are you ready?"[3]

Jackson's men surprised and routed General Oliver Otis Howard's XI Corps in the fields west of Chancellorsville. Jackson was anxious to press the attack and win a decisive victory. In an effort to achieve this and to scout the situation, Jackson, Boswell, and some others rode forward. The *Richmond Enquirer* reports:

> Gen. Jackson, having gone some distance in front of the line of skirmishers on Saturday evening (May 2), was returning about 8 o'clock attended by his staff and part of his couriers.
>
> The cavalcade was, in darkness of the night, mistaken for a body of the enemy cavalry, and fired upon by a regiment of his own corps. He was

struck by three balls—one through the left arm, two inches below the shoulder joint, shattering the bone and severing the chief artery; another ball passed between the elbow and wrist, making its exit through the palm of the hand; a third entered the palm of the right hand about the middle, passing through, and broke two bones. He was wounded on the plank road, about fifty yards in advance of the enemy. He fell from his horse and was caught by Capt. Wilbourn, to who he remarked, "All my wounds are by my own men."

Capt. Boswell was killed...Col. Crutchfield, chief of staff, was wounded by his side. Two couriers were killed. Lieuts. Morrison and Smith escaped uninjured.[4]

Enemy artillery fire was terrible at that moment. After falling from a litter when a bearer was shot, Jackson was left lying alone for about five minutes. He lost a large amount of blood, and later told Dr. McGuire that he thought he was going to bleed to death. He finally was placed in an ambulance and taken to a field hospital at Wilderness Run.

Hunter McGuire's account of the wounding, and the events that followed:

> Supported upon either side by his aides, Captains James Smith and Joseph Morrison, the General moved slowly and painfully toward the rear. Occasionally resting for a moment, to shake off the exhaustion which pain and the loss of blood produced, he at last reached the line of battle, where most of the men were lying down, to escape the shell and cannister, with which the Federals raked the road. General Pender rode up here to the little party, and asked who was wounded, and Captain Smith, who had been instructed by General Jackson to tell no one of his injury, simply answered "a Confederate officer"; but Pender recognized the General, and springing from his horse, hurriedly expressed his regret, and added that his lines were so much broken, he feared it would be necessary to fall back. At this moment the scene was a fearful one. The air seemed to be alive with the shrieks of shells and the whistling of bullets; horses, riderless and mad with fright, dashed in every direction; hundreds left the ranks and fled to the rear, and the groans of the wounded and dying, mingled with the wild shouts of others to be led again to the assault. Almost fainting as he was, from loss of blood, fearfully wounded, and as he thought, dying, Jackson was undismayed by this terrible scene. The words of Pender seemed to rouse him to life. Pushing aside the men who supported him, he stretched himself to his full height, and answered feebly, but distinctly enough to be heard above the din of the battle. Still more exhausted by this effort, he asked to be permitted to lie down for a few moments, but the danger from the fire, and capture by the Federal advance, was too imminent, and his aides, hurried him on. A litter having been obtained, he was placed upon it, and the bearers passed on as rapidly as the thick woods and rough ground permitted. Unfortunately, one of the bearers was struck down, and the litter having been supported at each of the four corners by a man, fell and threw

the General to the ground. The fall was a serious one, and as he touched the earth, he gave for the first time, expression to his suffering and groaned piteously.

Captain Smith sprang to his side, and as he raised his head, a bright beam of moonlight, made its way through the thick foliage and rested upon the pale face of the sufferer. The Captain was startled by its great pallor and stillness, and cried out, "Oh! General, are you seriously hurt?" "No," he answered, "don't trouble yourself, my friend, about me," and presently added something about winning the battle first, and attending to the wounded afterwards. He was placed upon the litter again, and carried a few yards, when I met with an ambulance. I knelt down by him, and said, "I hope you are not badly hurt, General." He replied very calmly, but feeble, "I am badly injured, Doctor; I fear I am dying." After a pause, he continued, "I am glad you have come." I think my wound in my shoulder is still bleeding. His clothes were saturated with blood, and hemorrhage was still going on from the wound. Compression of the artery with the finger arrested it, until lights being procured from the ambulance, the handkerchief which had slipped a little, was readjusted. His calmness amid the dangers which surrounded him, and at the supposed presence of death, and his uniform politeness, which did not forsake him, even under these, the most trying circumstances, were remarkable. His complete control, too, over his mind, enfeebled as it was by loss of blood, pain, &c., was wonderful. His suffering at this time was intense; his hands were cold, his skin clammy, his face pale, and his lips compressed and bloodless; not a groan escaped him—not a sign of suffering, except the slight corrugation of his brow, the fixed, rigid face, and the thin lips so tightly compressed that the impression of the teeth could be seen through them. Except these, he controlled by his iron will, all evidence of emotion, and more difficult than this even, he controlled that disposition to restlessness which many of us have observed upon the field of battle, attending great loss of blood. Some whiskey and morphia were procured form Dr. Straith, and administered to him, and placing him in the ambulance, it was started for the Corps Field Infirmary, at the Wilderness Tavern. Col. Crutchfield, his Chief of Artillery, was also in the ambulance. He had been wounded very seriously in the leg, and was suffering intensely.

The General expressed very feelingly, his sympathy for Crutchfield, and once, when the latter groaned aloud, he directed the ambulance to stop, and requested me to see if something could not be done for his relief. Torches had been provided, and every means taken to carry them to the hospital, as safely and easily as possible. I sat in the front part of the ambulance, with my finger resting upon the artery, above the wound, to arrest bleeding if it should occur. When I was recognized by acquaintances, and asked who was wounded, the General would tell me to say, "a Confederate officer." At one time, he put his right hand upon my head, and pulling me down to him, asked "if Crutchfield was dangerously wounded?" When I answered "No, only painfully hurt," he replied, "I am glad it is no worse." In a few moments after, Crutchfield did the same thing; and when he was told that the General was very seriously wounded, he groaned and cried out, "O, my God!" It was for this, that the General directed the ambulance to be halted, and requested that something should be done for Crutchfield's relief.

After reaching the hospital, he was placed in bed, covered with blankets, and another drink of whiskey and water given him. Two hours and a half elapsed before sufficient reaction took place, to warrant an examination. At two o' clock Sunday morning Surgeons Black, Walls and Coleman being present, I informed him that chloroform would be given him, and his wounds examined. I told him that amputation would probably be required, and asked if it was found necessary, whether it should be done at once. He replied promptly, "Yes, certainly; Doctor McGuire, do for me whatever you think best." Chloroform was then administered, and as he began to feel its effects, and its relief to the pain he was suffering, he exclaimed, "What an infinite blessing," and continued to repeat the word "blessing," until he became insensible. The round ball, which had lodged under the skin, upon the back of his right hand was extracted first. It had entered the palm, about the middle of the hand, and had fractured two of the bones. The left arm was then amputated, about two inches below the shoulder, very rapidly, and with slight loss of blood, the ordinary circular operation having been made. There were two wounds in this arm, the first and most serious was about three inches below the shoulder-joint, the ball dividing the main artery, and fracturing the bone. The second was several inches in length; a ball having entered the outside of the forearm, an inch below the elbow, came out upon the opposite side, just above the wrist. Throughout the whole of the operation, and until all the dressings were applied, he continued insensible. Two or three slight wounds of the skin on his face, received from the branches of trees, when his horse dashed through the woods, were dressed simply with isinglass plaster. About half past three o'clock Colonel (then Major) Pendleton, the Assistant Adjutant General, arrived at the hospital, and asked to see the General. He stated that Gen. Hill had been wounded, and that the troops were in great disorder. General Stuart was in command, and had sent him to see the General. At first, I declined to permit an interview, but the Colonel urged that the safety of the army and success of the cause depended upon his seeing him. When he entered the tent the General said, "Well, Major, I am glad to see you; I thought you were killed." Pendleton briefly explained the condition of affairs, gave Stuart's message, and asked what should be done. General Jackson was at once interested, and asked in his quick rapid way, several questions. When they were answered, he remained silent a moment, evidently trying to think; contracted his brow, set his mouth, and for some moments was obviously endeavoring to concentrate his thoughts. For a moment it was believed he has succeeded, for his nostrils dilated, and his eyes flashed its old fire, but it was only for a moment; his face relaxed again, and presently he answered very feebly and sadly, "I don't know—I can't tell; say to General Stuart he must do what he thinks best." Soon after this, he slept for several hours, and seemed to be doing well. The next morning he was free from pain, and expressed himself sanguine of recovery. He sent his aide-de-camp, Morrison, to inform his wife of his injuries, and to bring her at once to see him. The following note from General Lee, was read to him that morning by Captain Smith: "I have just received your note, informing me that you were wounded. I cannot express my regret at the occurrence. Could I have directed events, I should have chosen, for the good of the country, to have been disabled in your stead. I congratulate you upon the victory which is due to your skill and energy. He replied, "General Lee should give the praise to God." About ten o'clock his right side began to pain him so much that he asked me to examine it. He said he had injured it in falling from the litter the night before, and believed that he had struck it against a stone or the stump of a sapling. No evidence of injury could be discovered by examination; the skin was not broken or bruised, and the lung performed, as far as I could tell, its proper functions. Some simple application was recommended, in the belief that the pain would soon appear.

At this time the battle was raging fearfully, and the sound of the cannon and musketry could be distinctly heard at the hospital. The General's attention was attracted to it from the first, and when the noise was at its height, and indicated how fiercely the conflict was being carried on, he directed all of his attendants, except Captain Smith, to return to the battlefield, and attend to their duties. By eight o'clock, Sunday night, the pain in his side had disappeared, and in all respects he seemed to be doing well. He inquired minutely about the battle, and the different troops engaged, and his face would light up with enthusiasm and interest when told how this brigade acted, or that officer displayed conspicuous courage, and his head gave the peculiar shake from side to side, and he uttered his usual "Good, good," with unwonted energy when the gallant behavior of the "Stonewall Brigade" was alluded to. He said, "The men of that brigade will be, some day, proud to say to their children, 'I was one of the Stonewall Brigade.'" He disclaimed any right of his own to the name Stonewall. It belongs to the brigade and not to me.

This night he slept well, and was free from pain. A message was received from General Lee the next morning, directing me to remove the General to Guinea's Station, as soon as his condition would justify it, as there was some danger of capture by the Federals, who were threatening to cross at Ely's Ford. In the meantime, to protect the hospital, some troops were sent to this point. The General objected to being moved, if, in my opinion, it would do him any injury. He said he had no objection to staying in a tent, and would prefer it, if his wife, when she came, could find lodging in a neighboring house. "And if the enemy does come," he added "I am not afraid of them; I have always been kind to their wounded, and I am sure they will be kind to me." General Lee sent word again late that evening that he must be moved if possible, and preparations were made to leave the next morning. I was directed to accompany, and remain with him, and my duties with the corps, as medical director, were turned over to the Surgeon next in rank. General Jackson had previously declined to permit me to go with him to Guinea's, because complaints had been so frequently made of General officers, when wounded, carrying off with them the surgeons belonging to their commands. When informed of this order of the Commanding General, he said "General Lee has always been very kind to me, and I thank him." Very early Monday[5] morning he was placed in an ambulance and started for Guinea's Station, and about eight o'clock that evening he arrived at the Chandler House, where he remained till he died. Captain Hotchkiss, with a party of engineers, was sent in front to clear the road of wood, stone, etc., and to order the wagons out of the track to let the ambulance pass. The rough teamsters sometimes refused to move their loaded wagons out of the way for an ambulance, until told that it contained Jackson, and then, with all possible speed, they gave the way, and stood with hats off, and weeping, as he went by. At Spotsylvania C.H., and along the whole route, men and women rushed to the ambulance, bringing all the poor delicacies they had, and with tearful eyes they blessed him, and prayed for his recovery. He bore the journey well, and was cheerful throughout the day. He talked freely about the late battle, and among other things, said that he had intended to endeavor to cut the Federals off from the United States Ford, and taking a position between them and the river, oblige them to attack him; and he added, with a smile, "My men sometimes fail to drive the enemy from a position, but they always fail to drive us away." He spoke of Rodes, and alluded in high terms to his magnificent behavior of the field Saturday evening. He hoped he would be promoted. He thought promotions for gallantry should be made at once, upon the field, and not delayed; made very early, or upon the field, they would be the greatest incentives to gallantry in others. He spoke of Colonel Willis, who commanded the skirmishers of Rodes' Division, and praised him very highly, and referred to the death of Paxton and Boswell very feelingly. He alluded to them as officers of great merit and promise. The day was quite warm, and at one time he suffered with slight nausea. At his suggestion, I placed over his stomach a wet towel, and he expressed great relief from it. After he arrived at Chandler house, he ate some bread and tea with evident relish, and slept well throughout the entire night. Wednesday he was thought to be doing remarkable well. He ate heartily, for one in his condition, and was uniformly cheerful.

    I found his wounds to be doing very well to-day. Union by the first intention, had taken place, to some extent, in the stump, and the rest of the surface of the wound exposed, was covered with healthy granulations. The wound in his hand gave him little pain, and the discharge was healthy. Simple lime and water dressings were used both for the stump and hand, and upon the palm of the latter, a light, short splint was applied, to assist in keeping at rest the fragments of the second and third metacarpal bones. He expressed great satisfaction when told that the wounds were healing, and asked if I could tell from their appearance, how long he would probably be kept from the field? Conversing with Capt. Smith, a few moments afterwards, he alluded to his injuries, and said, "Many would regard them as a great misfortune, I regard them as one of the blessings of my life." Captain S. replied, "All things work together for good to those that love God." "Yes," he answered, "that's it, that's it."

At my request, Dr. Morrison came to-day, and remained with him.

About one o'clock Thursday morning while I was asleep upon a lounge in his room, he directed his servant, Jim, to apply a wet towel to his stomach, to relieve an attack of nausea, with which he was again troubled. The servant asked permission to first consult me, but the General knowing that I had slept none for nearly three nights, refused to allow the servant to disturb me, and found him suffering great pain. An examination disclosed pleuro-pneumonia of the right side. I believed, and the consulting physicians concurred in the opinion, that it was attributable to the fall from the litter the night he was wounded. The General, himself, referred it to this accident. I think the disease came on too soon after the application of the wet cloths, to admit of the supposition, once believed, that it was induced by them. The nausea, for which the cloths were applied that night, may have been the result of inflammation already begun. Contusion of the lung, with extravasation of blood in his chest, was probable produced by the fall referred to, and shock and loss of blood, prevented any ill effects until reaction had been well established, and then inflammation ensued. Cups were applied, and mercury, with antimony and opium administered. Towards the evening he became better, and hopes were again entertained of his recovery. Mrs. Jackson arrived to-day, and nursed him faithfully to the end. She was a devoted wife, and earnest Christian, and endeared us all to her by her great kindness and gentleness. The General's joy at the presence of his wife and child was very great, and for him unusually demonstrative. Noticing the sadness of his wife, he said to her tenderly, "I know you would gladly give your life for me, but I am perfectly resigned. Do not be sad; I hope I may yet recover. Pray for me, but always remember in your prayers to use the petition, "Thy will be done." Friday his wounds were again dressed, and although the quantity of the discharge from them, had diminished, the process of healing was still going on. The pain in his side had disappeared, but he breathed with difficulty and complained of a feeling of great exhaustion. When Dr. Breckinridge (who with Dr. Smith had been sent for in consultation) said he hoped that a blister, which had been applied, would afford him relief, he expressed his own confidence in it, and in his final recovery.

Dr. Tucker, from Richmond, arrived on Saturday, and all that human skill could devise was done, to stay the hand of death. He suffered no pain to-day, and his breathing was less difficult, but he was evidently hourly growing weaker.

When his child was brought to him, to-day, he played with it for some time; frequently caressing it, and calling it his "little comforter." At one time, he raised his wounded hand above its head, and closing his eyes, was for some moments, silently engaged in prayer. He said to me, "I see from the number of physicians that you think my condition is dangerous, but I thank God, if it is His will, that I am ready to go." About daylight, on Sunday morning, Mrs. Jackson informed him that his recovery was very doubtful, and that it was better that he should be prepared for the worst. He was silent for a moment, and then said: "It will be infinite gain to be translated to Heaven." He advised his wife, in the event of his death, to return to her father's house, and added, "You have a kind and good father, but there is no one so kind and good as your Heavenly Father." He still expressed a hope of his recovery, but requested her, if he should die, to have him buried in Lexington, in the Valley of Virginia. His exhaustion increased so rapidly that at eleven o'clock, Mrs. Jackson knelt by his bed, and told him that before the sun went down, he would be with his Savior. He replied, "Oh, no! you are frightened, my child; death is not so near; I may yet get well." She fell over upon the bed, weeping bitterly, and told him again that the physicians said there was no hope. After a moment's pause he asked her to call me. "Doctor, Anna informs me that you have told her that I am to die to-day; is it so?" When he was answered, he turned his eyes towards the ceiling, and gazed for a moment or two, as if in intense thought then replied, "Very good, very good, it is all right." He then tried to comfort his almost heart-broken wife, and told her he had a good deal to say to her, but he was too weak. Colonel Pendleton came into the room about one o'clock and he asked him, "Who was preaching at headquarters to-day?" When told that the whole army was praying for him, he replied, "Thank God—they are very kind." He said: "It is the Lord's Day; my wish is fulfilled. I have always desired to die on Sunday."

His mind now began to fail and wander, and he frequently talked as if in command upon the field, giving orders in his old way; then the scene shifted, and he was at the mess-table, in conversation with members of his staff; now with his wife and child; now at prayers with his military family. Occasional intervals of return of his mind would appear, and during one of them, I offered him some brandy and water, but he declined it, saying, "It will only delay my departure, and do no good; I want to preserve my mind, if possible, to the last." About half-past one, he was told that he had but two hours to live, and he answered again, feeble, but firmly, "Very good, it is all right." A few moments before he died he cried out in his delirium, "Order A.P. Hill to prepare for action! pass the infantry to the front rapidly! tell major Hawks"—then stopped, leaving the sentence unfinished. Presently, a smile of ineffable sweetness spread itself over his pale face, and he said quietly, and with an expression, as if of relief, "Let us cross over the river, and rest under the shade of the trees;" and then without pain, or the least struggle, his spirit passed from earth to God who gave it.[6]

# Chapter 13

Hunter McGuire's ordeal, which started late Saturday night, May 2, was over. Once again, as with little Janie Corbin, he had tried his best. But it was not enough. His friend Jackson was gone. Night and day he had sat by Jackson's bedside, treating him, listening to his breathing. Now it was over. As long as he lived, Hunter never forgot this week in May.

Soon, Union soldiers heard church bells tolling in Fredericksburg, tolling the death of the great Confederate captain. Sandie Pendleton rode to the telegraph office at Hamilton's Crossing and sent this message to Governor Letcher, "General Jackson died at fifteen minutes past 3 o'clock this afternoon. His remains will go to Richmond tomorrow."[7]

Sandie then returned to Chandler's and the office building to take charge of the funeral arrangements. Jackson, in accordance with his wishes, would be taken to Lexington for burial. The body was dressed by his aides, Sandie Pendleton and James P. Smith, and was placed in a rough coffin by the soldiers. Mrs. Jackson viewed his remains, realizing her Tom was gone. Dr. McGuire took stock of his thoughts too, and wondered what was ahead.

On Monday, May 11, 1863, the funeral train left Guiney's Station, south of Fredericksburg, for Richmond. Dr. McGuire was on the train, along with Mrs. Jackson and others on the staff. Crowds of people lined the tracks, and at Ashland some ladies placed wreathes and flowers on the casket.

Work was suspended in Richmond. The funeral train was expected at noon. A huge crowd gathered, but they were told the train would be in at four o'clock in the afternoon."[8] So they dispersed to regroup again late in the day.

The train stopped at the corner of Fourth and Broad to spare Mrs. Jackson the avalanche of mourners. Governor Letcher's wife met her and took her to the Letcher mansion. The casket was covered with the Confederate flag, evergreens, and other flowers. The hearse slowly started to move down Broad Street, flanked by Sandie Pendleton, Dr. McGuire, James P. Smith, and Henry Kyd Douglas. The procession continued to the governor's mansion[9] where the casket was to rest for the night. Pendleton and Douglas stood guard. The bells tolled until after sundown, as thousands of mourners thronged the square. The Richmond newspaper states that there had never been such an exhibition of "heartfelt and general sorrow" in the city.

Tuesday, May 12, was a lovely day in Richmond. Dr. McGuire and thousands of others greeted the dawn with breaking hearts. At ten o'clock in the morning, the funeral procession formed on the capitol grounds. The band of the Thirteenth Virginia Infantry led the marchers. Then came the military escort, followed by the hearse, which was draped and drawn by four white horses. Beside the hearse were the pallbearers: Sandie Pendleton, James P. Smith, Dr. Hunter McGuire, Henry Kyd Douglas, and six generals. After the hearse came the carriages with Jackson's family, President Jefferson Davis, and other dignitaries. Little Sorrel, Jackson's horse, was led by his personal attendant, Jim Lewis.[10]

Some of the musicians wept as they played. It was a very touching and moving moment. The casket was carried into the Senate Chamber, and there draped by the flag of the Confederacy, it lay in state until midnight.

That evening, Pendleton and Douglas went to the Tucker home. But Douglas left to return to the capitol for a "last, long, lingering look at his beloved general."[11] Earlier in the evening, Douglas, Pendleton, McGuire, Hawks, and Smith went to Mini's Photographic Gallery to have their pictures taken.

On May 13, a brief service was held in the governor's mansion. The citizens of Richmond hoped that Jackson would be buried in Hollywood Cemetery with their other great Virginians, but that was not his wish. Later in the day, the funeral train started from Richmond. On the train to Lynchburg was the Jackson family Pendleton, Smith, and McGuire of the general's staff.

At Lynchburg, Jackson was transferred to a packet boat, *The Marshall*, and the trip continued to Lexington. The grief-stricken group arrived in Lexington on May 14. Original plans called for burial on the sixteenth; however, Mrs. Jackson begged those in charge to move it ahead to the fifteenth. A detachment of VMI cadets stood guard over the casket as it rested in Jackson's former classroom.

On Friday, May 15, the funeral procession moved from the campus of VMI through the streets of Lexington to the Presbyterian Church. Mrs. Jackson and members of the staff followed on foot. Dr. William White, who had been Jackson's spiritual commander, was in charge of the brief service.

McGuire and the general's friendship had begun on the hills of Harpers Ferry. They had traveled to the Shenandoah Valley to Manassas, Sharpsburg, Fredericksburg, Chancellorsville, and Richmond. Now on a warm Friday in May, a young doctor from Winchester stood in the shadow of the everlasting hills by the grave of his friend and commander. Through the years he would extol the virtues of the man they called Stonewall.

Back home in Winchester many shops and businesses were closed to "those who would not take the Federal oath." There was even a rumor that the women of Winchester would be marched to church at the point of the bayonet on May 3. This was the day that Lincoln had set aside as a day of prayer and fasting.

Winchester rejoiced in the news of Hooker's defeat, but then came the news of the wounding of Jackson. Mrs. McDonald writes:

> ...our grief is almost as great as our joy, for no man was ever better loved by a people than Jackson; the inhabitants of the valley love and venerate him ardently, and...regard him...as their own...[12]

When the news of his death came, the people of Winchester regarded it as a personal tragedy. "The Mighty has fallen but he carries to his grave the hopes, and is followed by the bitter tears of the people in whose defense he lost his life....No loss could be felt as his will be....The Champion of the Valley is no more."[13]

# XIV

# With General Richard S. Ewell

The death of Stonewall Jackson necessitated a reorganization of the Army of Northern Virginia. General James Longstreet retained command of the First Corps. General Richard S. Ewell[1] was given command of the Second Corps, and General Ambrose P. Hill, the leadership of the newly created Third Corps.

During the last days of May 1863, Lee regrouped his infantry, rearmed the artillery, and refitted the cavalry. He knew now was the time to strike a major blow at the North. Men and materials were running low in the South, and if there was any hope for a final Southern victory, now was the hour.

Lee had a good psychological advantage. Despite Jackson's death, Northern morale was lower than that in the South. Some were clamoring for peace. And generals and men alike were outspoken in their criticism of Union military leadership. On the other hand, the Confederate soldiers believed that with their leaders they could not be defeated.

On May 29 a train arrived at Hamilton's Crossing carrying General Ewell. He had been selected to assume the responsibilities of the lamented Jackson. Ewell was returning to combat after losing a leg during the second battle of Manassas.

The army started north on June 5 with Culpeper as the first objective. The march over the next three weeks brought dusty roads, a heat wave, high humidity, then four days of rain. Dr. McGuire was busy treating the men for sore feet, cases of sunstroke, and heat exhaustion. And naturally, he had to supervise the movement of his ambulances, following the columns of infantry, cannon, caissons, and supply wagons.

From Culpeper, the Second Corps continued marching northward. By Saturday evening, June 13, Ewell was threatening Winchester from several directions and on Sunday, June 14, the city fell to Confederate troops.

After the fall of Winchester, Ewell asked Sandie Pendleton to prepare a message of congratulations for the troops. General Order No. 44 stated that the commanding general asked all the officers and men to join him in returning thanks to God for their success. Chaplains were asked to hold services of thanksgiving. A strong defensive work had been carried, three thousand prisoners captured, along with large quantities of military stores. "Such a result should strengthen the reliance in the righteousness of our cause, which has inspired every effort of our troops."[2]

Henry Kyd Douglas and Sandie Pendleton rode into Winchester. Henry writes:

> I found that the great joy of the people of that faithful town at their release was clouded by their grief at the death of General Jackson: every citizen of the town mourned as for a great personal bereavement.[3]

Pendleton also noted the grief among the joy. Writing to his beloved Kate, he said, "If the spirits disembodied can see what goes on in this world, I am sure that General Jackson has felt unfeigned pleasure since yesterday. 'Twas a sight worth seeing, the joy of the good people of Winchester as our men passed by yesterday at daylight. Old men and maidens vied with each other in demonstrations almost frantic."[4]

Sandie asked two young ladies to make a Confederate flag from two captured Union flags to fly over Fort Jackson, the new name of the fort north of town. He gave them new shoes captured from the Yankees as payment.

Cornelia McDonald and most of Dr. McGuire's friends in Winchester despised Union General Robert H. Milroy. Yet in a strange twist of emotion as Mrs. McDonald saw him leave town with his escort, fleeing from General Jubal Early, she felt sorry for him. He looked very agitated. His military career was finished. She bowed to him, and he returned the gesture.[5] While shells flew overhead, the wounded were brought to the McDonald porch. The children thought everybody would be killed. But at sundown, the firing ceased. And Mrs. McDonald heated milk for the wounded.

On the sixteenth, Mrs. McDonald helped make a new Confederate flag. She saw General Jubal A. Early as the flag was taken to the star fort and unfurled to the breezes of the Shenandoah Valley. During the day, Dr. McGuire told her the news that General Micah Jenkins was already in Pennsylvania.[6]

General Lee was supposed to be in Winchester on June 18, but Mrs. McDonald did not get to see him because of the heavy rain; however, she was the recipient of a captured Union mess chest, compliments of General Early.[7]

From his hometown, Dr. McGuire rode northward to Martinsburg, across the Potomac, and to Williamsport, Maryland. General Robert Rodes and his men had crossed on the sixteenth and were now encamped near Hagerstown.

Several days later, the residents of Chambersburg, Pennsylvania, heard music. Coming from the south end of town could be heard the strains of "The Bonnie Blue Flag," and "Dixie." Confederate infantry came marching up Main Street. The Confederate flag replaced the national flag on the pole in the public square, and General Ewell and staff established headquarters in the woods surrounding the Mennonite Church, just north of town.

Pendleton took time to go shopping. From headquarters he wrote, "My dear Mother, As I have spent all the money I have in the world —in buying dry goods for you and the girls, and expect to send them back to Winchester to Dr. McGuire's this afternoon, I write to let you know the facts and to enclose the bill."[8]

Around eleven o'clock on the morning of Saturday, June 27, the advance guard of the Confederate army entered Carlisle. They were now less than 20 miles from Harrisburg, the capital of Pennsylvania. A few more miles and a victory on the banks of the Susquehanna and perhaps there would be final victory for the South. The men were in excellent spirits, believers in themselves and in victory for their cause.

About 5 P.M. General Ewell and his staff rode into Carlisle, while his bands played "Dixie." The Second Corps, Army of Northern Virginia, was riding the crest of the invasion. General Ewell, who had been stationed at Carlisle earlier in his career, took quarters at the army barracks. He sent men into town to secure medical instruments and supplies for Dr. McGuire and the other physicians with his command. He sought amputating equipment and chloroform.[9]

By night fall, Confederate troops filled the grounds of the Carlisle military post and the campus of Dickinson College.[10] The cavalry was pushing on to scout Harrisburg and its defenses from the banks of the Susquehanna River. This last Saturday in June was a great day for McGuire and the men in General Rodes' division.

Dr. McGuire believed firmly in states' rights and was deeply committed to Virginia. At times he could become very temperamental when either one was questioned. One of the happy moments of his life occurred in Carlisle when he saw the flag of the Confederacy flying in the North. After the flag-raising ceremony,[11] Dr. McGuire, Sandie Pendleton, and two fellow officers secured passes to enter town to attend church. They went to the Presbyterian Church. Those in attendance were mainly Southern soldiers. There was no mention of the war when the minister prayed for Divine guidance for all in authority. After the service, it was discovered that the pastor was from Alabama.

Other units of the Second Corps were camped at the Dickinson College campus. Most of the professors were cordial; however, the teacher of chemistry enraged Pendleton and McGuire. The professor justified the burning of Darien, Georgia, by the Yankees. McGuire was angry enough to confiscate his chemistry equipment.[12] The Yanks had taken equipment from William and Mary College. Pendleton and McGuire wanted revenge.

McGuire, Pendleton, and Douglas felt honored to be a member of the Second Corps of the Army of Northern Virginia. Sandie compared it to the privilege of being a member of the famed Roman legions. "Thank God for being a part of it. I'd rather be here than anywhere else." So felt Pendleton and McGuire.[13]

On Monday, June 29, the Confederate Second Corps was recalled by General Lee to rejoin the rest of the army at a place called Gettysburg. Ewell was furious at being unable to carry out his mission. McGuire was disappointed, but the Union army was in Frederick, Maryland, under a new leader, General George G. Meade. The high hopes of the Confederates had to be abandoned.

Monday evening, the soldiers of the Confederacy and the citizens of Carlisle mingled around the campfires of the soldiers. The troops had been well behaved.[14] The residents had no bad feelings against the soldiers. They thought of their own relatives in the military and asked questions about the cause of the conflict. All expressed the hope that the war would soon be over.

At midnight they parted company. Some of the young ladies cried, and the hearts of the young soldiers from the South were full, too. They had miles and miles to go and a battle to fight, and perhaps suffering and death were on the horizon. When they spoke their final words, they said, "Good night, and God help us all."

On Tuesday, June 30, McGuire and his ambulances followed Ewell and Rodes to Mt. Holly Springs and to Middletown. General Henry Heth of Hill's Third Corps had asked permission to enter Gettysburg in the morning to look for shoes.

With the dawn of July 1, Heth's men left their camps near Cashtown, west of Gettysburg. Awaiting them on a range of hills called Seminary Ridge were the troopers of General John Buford's cavalry. A heavy engagement followed as both sides called for reinforcements. Among these answering the summons was the Union I Corps at Marsh Creek, south of Gettysburg, and the Confederate infantry of Rodes north of the town. At the conclusion of their marches, they met in combat on Oak Ridge. Losses were heavy, and Dr. McGuire faced hours of exhausting work with the wounded.

Union resistance was swept aside. Lee's army, being closer to Gettysburg, was able to bring more troops into action. The other divisions of Ewell's Corps arrived. Edward Johnson came from Chambersburg, and Jubal Early from York. The Union I and XI Corps were pushed back to Cemetery Hill outside of the town.

Ewell made his headquarters at the Culp home at the east side of Gettysburg. McGuire was most likely with him or nearby in a field hospital. The Confederate Second Corps was ready to launch a major attack on Culp's Hill and Cemetery Ridge. Now was the time, with victory in sight. But Ewell had no orders, and he would not commit his troops to the attack. Pendleton and Douglas[15] lamented the fact that Jackson was not there. McGuire undoubtedly concurred in this feeling. But no attack was made, and the advantage was lost.

Bitter fighting followed on July 2, and then came Pickett's ill-fated charge on July 3. Among the wounded was McGuire's friend Henry Kyd Douglas. He was hit in the left shoulder, tearing his coat, shirt, and undershirt. These items were imbedded in the shoulder. For a while some of the muscles in the left arm were paralyzed. Douglas was taken to the rear, to a home in Hunterstown.

When McGuire treated Henry he said, "I'm glad to see that you are not going to die as I heard you were. Our old crowd is getting too small. I'll leave Dr. Taney for you and the men in the barn..."[16]

With the repulse of Pickett's Charge, the retreat to Virginia was inevitable. Lee could not stay in Pennsylvania. Brigadier General John Imboden was ordered to report to Lee. Lee said to Imboden, "We must get back to Virginia. As many of our poor wounded as possible must be taken home." Imboden was given the task of guiding and guarding the wagon train of wounded. Imboden describes the agony and the plight of the wounded on Saturday, July 4, 1863.

> Shortly after noon the very windows of heaven seemed to have been opened. Rain fell in dashing torrents, and in a little while the whole face of the earth was covered with water. The meadows became small lakes, raging streams ran across the road in every depression of the ground. The storm increased in fury every moment, canvas was no protection against it, and the poor wounded lying upon the hard, naked boards of the wagon-bodies were drenched by the cold rain. Horses and mules were blinded and maddened by the storm and became almost unmanageable. The roar of the winds and waters made it almost impossible to communicate orders; night was rapidly approaching and there was danger that in the darkness and in the confusion the horses would become "confounded."
>
> At about 4:00 p.m. the head of the column was put in motion and began the ascent of the mountain. The train was seventeen miles long when drawn out on the road. It was moving rapidly and from every wagon issued wails of agony. For four hours I galloped along, passing to the front and heard more—it was too dark to see—of the horrors of war than I had witnessed from the battle of Bull Run to that day. In the wagons were men wounded and mutilated in every conceivable way. Some had their legs shattered by a shell or Minié ball; some were shot in the face, or a jagged piece of shell had lacerated their heads.
>
> Scarcely one in a hundred had received adequate surgical aid; and many had been without food for thirty-six hours.
>
> Their ragged, dirty, and bloody clothes, all clotted and hardened with blood, were rasping the tender, inflamed lips of their gaping wounds. Very few of the wagons has even straw in them, and all were without springs. The road was rough and rocky. The jolting was enough to have killed strong, sound men. From nearly every wagon as the horses trotted along such cries and shrieks as these greeted the ears:
>
> "My God! Will no one have mercy and kill me, and end my misery?"

### RETREAT FROM GETTYSBURG

It is uncertain whether McGuire was with the wagon train, or whether he was with Ewell and the rest of the Second Corps. Normally, he would have been with the headquarters staff; however, with a wagon train 17 miles long, he may have been assisting in the care of these men. The agony of the wounded was witnessed throughout the countryside.

> "O God! Why can't I die?"
>
> "Oh! stop one minute, take me out and leave me by the roadside to die."
>
> "I am dying! I am Dying! Oh, my poor wife and children! What will become of you?"
>
> Some were praying, others were uttering the most fearful oaths and imprecations that despair could wring from them in their agony....[17]

Lee could not cross the Potomac for nearly two weeks. The river was at flood stage, and the army was unable to cross until the night of July 13; however, a flatboat, hooked to a cable, transported some of the wounded to the Virginia shore and brought supplies across to the army. McGuire may have remained in Williamsport, Maryland, with the army, or he perhaps traveled to Winchester to supervise hospital work there.

Originally the news reaching Winchester indicated that the Confederate army had won a great victory at Gettysburg. Long lines of captive Union soldiers being sent to Staunton seemed to verify the news. There had also been a continuous flow of cattle, hogs, and wagons filled with Pennsylvania produce. Then around July 7 came the dreadful truth. Some segments of General Imboden's wagon train of wounded started arriving in Winchester. It was a pathetic sight. Many of the residents of Winchester wondered how long General Lee could endure.

> Uncertainty and dread of the evil to come seemed to fill every heart; preparations were going forward to evacuate the town again, and all was confusion and distress...The whole town seemed to be trying the get away; everything that had wheels was in demand and even a cart was deemed a prize.[18]

Like her friends and neighbors, Cornelia McDonald had to face reality. Taking the advice of the older men, she loaded a few possessions and her family in a wagon. She left her beloved Winchester, a refugee, heading for Lexington. "The sun was just rising....We...left the old town far behind....This was just the beginning of our sorrows."[19]

The Army of Northern Virginia spent the remainder of July in the Winchester area. Many soldiers stopped at the McGuire home. Among them were Jed Hotchkiss and Hunter when he had a few moments.

In late August, Sandie Pendleton was promoted to the rank of lieutenant colonel.[20] This was quite an achievement for a young man not yet 23 years of age. Sandie also became chief of staff for the Second Corps.

Dr. Robert L. Dabney[21] visited headquarters in September. He was anxious to begin a book on the life of Stonewall Jackson, so he came and took notes from McGuire, Pendleton, and others. On Saturday night, September 5, Dabney and McGuire spent a long session together discussing the life and contributions of Jackson.

In mid-October, Lee and Meade clashed at Bristoe Station. This time the Confederate leadership was poor and General Hill along with General Ewell received a lot of criticism. Their actions even caused Lee to get angry.

On November 7, Meade surprised the Confederates and inflicted heavy losses on them at Rappahannock Station. Once again, the staff of the Second Corps lamented the loss of Jackson and the current ineffective leadership. Lee then placed Ewell's Corps along the Rapidan River from Orange Court House to Mine Run.

Ewell established his headquarters at Morton Hall, near Raccoon Ford. Mrs. Ewell and her daughter moved in with them, upsetting Dr. McGuire. Army headquarters was no place for a woman, and besides, he was very fond of Mrs. Ewell.

# Chapter 14

McGuire was also angered by the way the farmers and villagers had been treated by the Yankees. The Union soldiers had taken food, clothing, and furniture from many homes. They had behaved very poorly and treated the Virginians very badly.

McGuire's spirits were lifted a little in November when his brother Hugh paid a visit to Morton Hall. Many officers came for a conference, and Hugh accompanied by his commander spent time with Hunter.

On November 16, Sandie Pendleton received a letter from his betrothed, Kate Corbin. The contents were so important that Sandie asked for a leave and rode to Moss Neck. The Corbins were in mourning. Richard Corbin, the owner of Moss Neck, had been killed in action near Culpeper on September 13. Kate was distressed over the anguish of her sister Berrie. First, Janie had died, now Richard. It was hard to think of getting married while surrounded with all this sadness. The wedding, originally scheduled for October 23, had already been postponed once. Now, Kate was thinking about another postponement. A personal visit from Sandie, however, relieved her fears, and after a long talk they set a date for later in November. Returning to Morton Hall, Sandie stopped and prayed at the spot where Jackson had fallen.

On November 23, Moss Neck manor, the estate where Jackson and his men had spent a happy winter, was advertised for sale in the *Richmond Daily Enquirer*.[22] The real estate advertisement noted that it contained 676 valuable acres and improvements. Regardless, Sandie and Kate went ahead with plans for their wedding.

This time an advance by General Meade prevented Pendleton and McGuire from leaving camp. The women were all gathered at Moss Neck and everything was ready, but the soldiers were missing. Once again, the wedding was postponed.

Living in the midst of war and uncertainty, touched by the things that had happened to Kate, and the postponement of their marriage, Sandie thought of the past and wrote to Kate on November 25, 1863:

> A bright fire blazes behind me and it is as comfortable as need be in a canvas house; my carpet is a rich green sod and my only furniture consists of a valise, a pile of blankets, a pair of holsters, some old clothes hanging from the ridge pole, my folding camp table, and the stool on which I am sitting. The stool is one of the relics cherished by our mess.
>
> It belonged to our dear friends, Gen'l Jackson and we, Smith, McGuire and I, cling fondly to everything that reminds us of him, and glory in our title of the 'Jackson Club,' as we are called by the rest of our military family...Oh! how often have I set by Gen'l Jackson as we gathered around the camp fire, and joined in cheerful conversation. A regular happy family we were in those days. Ah, the circle is broken up, some gone with him to their long rest, some languishing with wounds, and some others still left here on our duty at our posts, ready, I trust, to do or suffer what is always allotted us by Providence.[23]

Sandie stated that he had a legacy of "pleasure and pride...in the remembrance of long service" with Jackson, and was proud of the fact that he enjoyed Jackson's "love and confidence."[24] Sandie, indeed, was like a son, and many compared the moral and devotional life of the young officer with Jackson's. Many questioned who prayed more, Jackson or Pendleton.

Concluding his thought, Sandie said, "One thing I know, I am a better soldier and a better man for having associated so long and intimately with Gen'l Jackson; and I know also, in which knowledge you are interested, that I shall make you a better husband and that is my chief anxiety now."[25]

November 25 had been the date for the wedding. But the Second Corps now had a new commander, making it doubly important for Sandie to be in camp. General Ewell was sick in a Charlottesville hospital. Jubal Early was now in command. And Kate realized "It will be tough to get a furlough. He is so opposed to wives and matrimony."[26]

On December 4, Sandie wrote his father that barring the resumption of fighting, he would apply for a leave on December 14 and be married on December 16. Once again, things were made ready at Moss Neck, the house was cleaned, and "the fatted calf was killed."[27] Alas, no groom arrived. Sandie was riding with General Early to check on conditions in the Shenandoah Valley.

Dr. William N. Pendleton almost gave up on the possibility of the December wedding and returned to visit his family in Lexington. He had not been home since August 1861. Just after his arrival he received a telegram from Sandie saying that he had obtained a furlough and expected to be married December 29 at Moss Neck. Pendleton stayed with his wife and family until after the Christmas dinner. Then he took a buggy through a snowstorm to Staunton where he boarded a train for Richmond. He arrived on the twenty-eighth.

Kate was even more surprised than Dr. Pendleton. Sandie, after the last postponement, had told Kate to stand by. On December 27 he arrived at Moss Neck and said he expected to be married on the twenty-ninth.

On December 28, Sandie traveled to Richmond to meet his father, Reverend Pendleton, Hunter McGuire, and James P. Smith. En route he stopped at Bowling Green, the county seat of Caroline County, for his marriage license.[28]

The men did not arrive back at Moss Neck until December 29. With the Reverend Dr. Pendleton officiating, Sandie and Kate finally took their marital vows attended by McGuire and Smith.

Although McGuire was very happy for Sandie, and he was fond of Kate, the marriage left still another gap in his life. The year of 1863 had been a very tough one for Sandie. First, his servant Jim had died, then Janie Corbin, followed by Jackson and Boswell. Now, his tent mate was a married man.

There was a positive note though. Sandie and Kate had been observing the growing relationship between McGuire and Mary Stuart, daughter of A. H. H. Stuart of Staunton. Sandie notes: "McGuire is beginning to learn that love is not a matter of head only, but of the heart and soul."[29] By May 1864, Hunter McGuire was engaged to Mary Stuart; however, with the uncertainties of war, the young couple decided to wait until later to get married.

# The Year of 1864

"On to Richmond," this was the objective of the Northern politicians and generals in the early days of the war. Several attempts had been made, all ending in failure for the North. Fredericksburg, 50 miles south of Washington, had the misfortune of being located on the Rappahannock River, midway between Washington and Richmond. Fredericksburg already had suffered from two Union attempts to move on Richmond, the battles of Fredericksburg in December 1862, and Chancellorsville in May 1863. As the days grew longer and spring arrived along the banks of the Rappahannock, it was time to break camp and get ready for another campaign.

Dr. McGuire was serving under his third commander in a year. He entered the war as a private soldier in the Second Virginia. Then he became the surgeon for the First Brigade under Jackson, followed by medical director for the Second Corps. Now, Ewell was to be replaced by Jubal A. Early,[1] and McGuire's title would be medical director, Army of the Valley. Before Early assumed command at the end of May, McGuire would have to treat many men wounded from the savage fighting in a tangled growth of deep woods known as the Wilderness, 17 miles west of Fredericksburg.

Shortly after midnight on May 4, 1864, the Army of the Potomac, comprised of over one hundred thousand men, started moving from their winter quarters near Culpeper, Virginia, heading for the Rapidan River. The Union army had another new leader, General Ulysses Simpson (Unconditional Surrender) Grant. In March, President Lincoln named Grant commander in chief of all the armies of the United States, with headquarters in the east with the Army of the Potomac.

Grant's concept of war was different from that of Robert E. Lee. The Confederate leader followed the theories of Napoleon, that the key to military success was winning a war with a single, major victory. Grant's idea was to hammer the enemy and to keep him constantly engaged, wearing him out, then breaking through his lines and destroying him. The battles of the Wilderness and Spotsylvania Court

House resulted from the moves and theories of General Grant. Losses on both sides were heavy. McGuire was kept very busy treating the wounded of the Second Corps.

Grant continued his forward movements, and on May 30, General Gouverneur K. Warren's Union V Corps fought the Confederates at Bethesda Church, northeast of Mechanicsville. During the battle, Colonel Edward Willis,[2] a fellow officer on Jackson's staff and temporarily in command of the brigade, was mortally wounded.

Sandie and others found McGuire by the bedside of a dying comrade:

> I found him evidently dying, but not suffering much pain, and perfectly conscious. Dr. McGuire, Medical Director of this corps, was with him, and as I came to the pallet where he lay, (McGuire) said, "Ned, here's Sandy Pendleton come to see you." Ned opened his eyes, and grasped my hand with both of his, and said, "Sandy, the doctors won't tell me whether I am going to die. Am I mortally wounded?" I replied, "Yes, Ned, I am afraid you are mortally wounded." He said, "That's right old fellow, that's the way I like to hear a man talk. I am not afraid to die any more than I was afraid to go into battle." I said, "Ned, I trust you have as good cause not to fear death as you had not to fear the enemy." To which he replied, "I trust so, Sandy, I believe I have."
>
> After a short pause Dr. McGuire said, "Ned, I did not tell you you were going to die, because there is chance for your recovery, but it is so slim a chance as almost to amount to none, and I did not want you to build hopes on it." Ned replied, "I am very glad that there is a chance to get well, but I am not afraid to die. Doctor, if I die will it be today, and will I suffer much pain?" The doctor said he would probably die during the day and without much pain, which satisfied him. He then asked Dr. M. minutely as to the course of the bullet, and seemed satisfied when it was described.
>
> Hearing that he wished to see Lt. Col. Moxley Sorrel of Longstreet's staff I told Ned he has been sent for. He thanked me and I asked him if there was anyone else he wanted to see. He said, "Yes, Moxley Sorrel's sister to whom I am betrothed. I am not afraid to die. I don't mind it myself, but it will almost break her heart and my poor father's and mother's. Tell her not to be distressed. I die in the best cause a man could fall in." He said nothing more, but seemed a good deal moved. After a few moments he asked me to see that all his debts were paid by Capt. Reed, Quartermaster of his regt. The Doctor here interfered to give him some brandy and said that some ice and strawberries would be good for him; I left and sent him some.[3]

Grant was not like the other Union commanders. Instead of retreating after the battles of the Wilderness and Spotsylvania, he headed south, causing a race as Lee tried to stay between Grant and Richmond. As a result the siege of Petersburg started in the summer of 1864 and lasted until the following spring.

# Chapter 15

As Grant closed in on Richmond, the Union army made another thrust in the Shenandoah Valley. General Franz Sigel was defeated by the Confederates at New Market on May 15. Sigel was replaced by General David Hunter, who pushed down to Lexington and then on to Lynchburg.

To relieve pressure on Richmond and Lynchburg, Lee detached Old Jubal Early for special duty. His assignment was to meet and defeat Hunter, clear the Valley, cross the Potomac, and threaten Washington. It was hoped that this action by Early would cause Grant to transport troops from Petersburg to defend Washington.

Early was a good fighter and a good division commander, but he was to receive a lot of criticism as a corps commander. His division commanders for this special mission were Generals John B. Gordon, John C. Breckinridge, and Robert Rodes.

The troops left their positions in the trenches surrounding Richmond on Monday, June 13. Two days later they were at Louisa Court House. They could still be called "Jackson's Foot Cavalry" as they covered 65 miles in two days. The next day was even worse, 28 miles—destination Charlottesville. The men were informed that they were going to attack General David Hunter's troops at Lynchburg. Trains were waiting to take them from Charlottesville to Lynchburg. But the trains broke down and the march continued.

Lynchburg was saved, and then it was on to Lexington. Here the Stonewall Brigade, McGuire, Pendleton, and Douglas paid homage to General Jackson. It was a touching moment. Douglas writes:

> When we entered Lexington, Jackson's old division was marched by his grave. Not a man spoke, not a sound was uttered. Only the tramp, tramp of passing feet told that his surviving veterans were passing in review while the drooping and tattered flags saluted his sacred dust.[4]

Douglas, released from captivity and after a bout with an illness, was happy to be back with his comrades. General Hunter had left a path of destruction in the Shenandoah Valley. This infuriated McGuire and Douglas. Henry felt that this was a case "where vengeance should not be left entirely to the Lord."

On July 2, Early's marching columns reached Winchester where they received a joyous welcome. An entry in Jed Hotchkiss's diary reads, "The people of Winchester were so glad to see us and as loyal as ever."[5]

Most of the Confederate column crossed the Potomac River at Shepherdstown. Douglas took Generals Early, Breckinridge, Gordon, and Ramseur to visit his Ferry Hill home.

The Confederate advance split into three columns. The infantry crossed South Mountain heading eastward with Rodes using Turner's Gap, Breckinridge taking his troops through Fox's Gap, and Gordon using Crampton's Gap to the south.

Early was also disturbed over the manner in which General Hunter and his Union troops had treated the residents of the Shenandoah Valley. Early, therefore, was determined to ransom the Maryland cities. Thus Hagerstown, Middletown, and Frederick were threatened, and Confederate General John McCausland laid the torch to Chambersburg.

General Early asked the citizens of the village of Middletown for $5,000. They told him the money was unavailable. He stuck to his demands, and the villagers collected $1,500 while the farmers contributed another $3,500. Early's staff considered giving this money to the farmers who had been victimized in the Shenandoah Valley.

Frederick was a larger place, having a population of nearly eight thousand. General Early and his staff entered the city and went to the home of Dr. and Mrs. Hammond located at the northwest corner of North Market and Second Streets. The Hammonds reportedly were Confederate sympathizers. Early asked for some writing materials, thought for a few moments, and wrote a note. When he finished he turned to Mrs. Hammond and said:

> Madam, we are going to make a demand upon the banks of Frederick for $200,000, and if the demand is granted, very good, if not, Frederick will be reduced to ashes. We do this in retaliation for similar acts done by Federal soldiers within our borders. You need not fear, as timely warning will be given to you to leave with your family.[6]

The paper was signed by Colonel William Allan, chief of ordnance; Major Wells J. Hawks, chief of commissary; Dr. Hunter McGuire, surgeon and medical director; and Major John Harman, chief quartermaster.[7]

The demand was for the $200,000 in cash, but the city could comply by bringing $50,000 worth of supplies to the medical department, along with $50,000 in stores and supplies for ordnance, commissary, and quartermaster departments. Major Hawks also requested 500 barrels of flour, 6,000 pounds of sugar, 3,000 pounds of salt, 3,000 pounds of coffee, and 20,000 pounds of bacon.

Mayor William Cole and a group of lawyers considered the demands. They thought it was very unreasonable and asked to have it reduced to more realistic figures. Early refused to heed their pleas.

Early had no time to waste. Union reinforcements were gathering on the banks of the Monocacy River[8] south of Frederick. He sent Pendleton to make sure the mayor and the lawyers were working on the problem, and told them to "hurry." Five banks in the city of Frederick pooled their resources to meet Early's demands. Major Braithwaite of the quartermaster department gave Mayor Cole a receipt "in full payment." How the money was divided is uncertain.

Later in the day heavy action occurred on the banks of the Monocacy. Troops under Gordon and Breckinridge were fully engaged. The heat and the combat took a heavy toll, and Dr. McGuire was very busy. He had to leave about four hundred wounded in Frederick when the army resumed its march toward Washington. General Grant said later that as Major General Lew Wallace "fought for time," his action saved Washington from capture. And years later General, now senator, Gordon stated that "Wallace's action snatched Washington from Confederate hands." Some say this was the battle that saved the Union.

During the evening, Pendleton, back in the city of his boyhood days, celebrated the Confederate victory with Allan, Hawks, and Harman over a "delicious dish of ice cream."[9] McGuire was not with them; no doubt he was with the wounded.

General Early's forces reached the gates of Washington. The Confederate threat brought terror and alarm to the national government. President Lincoln came out to Fort Stevens to watch the action. He was told to take cover and was almost hit by a shot. The Confederate advance was a bold, daring action against great odds, and it almost succeeded. The odds, however, were too great for Early to overcome. He had to withdraw. Recrossing the Potomac, Early and his troops operated in the Martinsburg-Winchester area and sparred with Union troops under General Philip H. Sheridan for the rest of the summer.

The march to the gates of Washington had made General Grant realize that as long as Confederate forces were in the northern end of the Shenandoah Valley, an invasion was possible and food would be available to the South. Thus, Grant and Sheridan met at the Thomas farm south of Frederick and made plans to eradicate Early's army and the granary of the Shenandoah Valley. By early August, large Union reinforcements were gathering at Harpers Ferry. Among them were the VI Corps, which Grant had sent from the trenches of Petersburg under General Horatio Gouverneur Wright, George Crook's division of the XIX Corps, and Alfred Torbert's division of cavalry. This force numbered 40,000 men, and Sheridan called it the Army of the Shenandoah.

Opposing this Union army were Early's divisions under John Breckinridge, John B. Gordon, Robert Rodes, and Stephen Ramseur. Early had about 8,500 infantry, and approximately 3,600 artillery and cavalrymen.

Stephen Dodson Ramseur, a native of North Carolina, was a brigadier general in Early's army. Recently married and only 27 years of age in the summer of 1864, he was one of McGuire's friends. Ramseur wrote to his wife saying he hoped the invasion of Maryland might bring hopeful results for their cause. Even in late August, he thought peace might come. Ramseur and many of his comrades were hoping that McClellan, the Democratic candidate for president, and the Peace Party might prevail in the November elections in the North. They may have, had Ramseur and his men been able to defeat Sheridan in the Valley. Ramseur assured his wife:

> Every man whose opinion I have asked and who has had an opportunity of learning the feelings of the Yankee people and soldiery, assures me that the North is tired of war and will elect an out and out, unconditional peace man at the Presidential election....I trust these opinions may be verified.[10]

In September, Sherman defeated Hood and captured Atlanta. This was great news for Lincoln, and foreboding news for McGuire. As Ramseur said, "Our hopes for peace depend upon the success of our armies in the field." The McClellan platform was constructed to depend on events in the field. Ramseur was sure, "If our armies can hold their own, suffer no crushing disaster before the next election, we may reasonably expect a termination of this war."

From the camp near Winchester, Ramseur wrote to his wife on September 11.

> We have enjoyed a great variety of scenes—have travelled over and sojourned in the most beautiful part of the valley of Va....We consider

ourselves very fortunate thus far....I wish you could see this magnificent Valley—at this beautiful season of the year. Although plantations are ruined and blackened remains at once splendid mansions are to be seen on all sides yet nature is triumphant—magnificent meadows, beautiful forests and broad undulating fields rich in grass and clover! Truly it does seem sacrilegious to despoil such an Eden! by the ravages of war.

I thank God that my loved ones have not yet known the terror and wretchedness caused by the presence of our mean cowardly foes, Foes who respect not helpless Age nor tender women. Surely as just God will visit upon such a nation the just indication of His wrath![11]

Ramseur believed Early's army was doing well in holding 40,000 and 50,000 Union troops and neutralizing their use. Early's army was gathering the wheat to send to Lee's army and also supplying themselves with the beef from the area. He was happy to realize that the Union held less of Virginia than any time since 1862.

On September 17, Grant and Sheridan met in Charles Town, near Harpers Ferry, to plan their strategy. Sheridan explained that the Opequon Creek was a barrier, a natural defensive work for the Confederates, but that he was now ready. Critics felt Sheridan had taken too long to get ready. But his preparations and ensuing actions did more in six weeks than previous commanders had done in three years.

On September 19, Sheridan moved westward along the Berryville Pike and attacked the Confederate troops entrenched along the Opequon Creek. Things were going well for Early, and it looked like Sheridan would be turned back. But then the report went up that Union cavalry had brushed aside Confederates north of Winchester and that the main line was being outflanked. Rodes was struck by a shell fragment and mortally wounded. The Confederate line broke and ran.

Sheridan's infantry pressed them back through the streets of Winchester. Mrs. John B. Gordon was staying in town. Hearing the commotion, she ran into the street and tried to rally the troops. She was almost run down by the soldiers and captured.

Early continued his retreat to Strasburg and beyond to Fisher's Hill, "which he considered the only place suitable to make a stand against Sheridan." Early had lost 3,611 men at Winchester and inflicted heavy losses on Sheridan. "Little Phil" had replacements, whereas Jubal Early did not.

Early lost a fine officer in Robert Rodes,[12] who could not be replaced. Also among the fallen was Colonel George S. Patton who was mortally wounded and left behind in Union hands.

Sheridan called this battle Opequon to distinguish it from other actions. In this engagement, Sheridan "restored the lower valley to Union control, from which it was never again wrested; it permanently relieved Maryland and Pennsylvania from the periodical invasions to which they had been subjected during three years, and the national capital from further humiliation."[13]

The victory had a profound psychological impact on the North. At last someone had won a Union victory in the Shenandoah Valley. Faith and hope were restored. The charisma of the young commander spread throughout the country and among his troops. The men had confidence in themselves and in their leader. The attention of the nation turned to the Shenandoah Valley. What happened in the next few weeks south of Winchester would help to determine who would win the November election.

General Early regrouped at Fisher's Hill, the first strong line of resistance south of Winchester. "Here the main Valley, twenty miles wide below, narrows to four."[14] He was barely in position before Sheridan struck. Little John Fisher saw his aged grandfather knocked down by a Union trooper. He saw the family's mill set on fire, machinery broken, and hauled away. And when the flames leaped skyward, he scraped up some flour for his mother and his eleven brothers and sisters. Once again, the Confederates were overwhelmed. Early's left flank was "turned, driven back, and routed…We were driven from the field in great disorder."

Sandie Pendleton rode back to check the rear guard. Douglas says:

> He was riding a white horse, and I warned him against riding such a beast on such a night. He made some light remark about 'the deadly white horse,' and rode along the skirmish line which was falling back very slowly….We stopped for a minute, when Pendleton gave a groan and tottered forward on his horse. I dismounted, called a man or two; he fell gently into my arms and was taken from his horse. He tried to walk but could not get far and, just then, the man on the opposite side from me was shot and he sank to the ground. Several strong men helped carry him to the rear as the enemy's fire became galling. I had sent for an ambulance and when it arrived he was placed in it. He was shot in the groin and through the body. He told me he was mortally wounded. He gave me his watch, pocketbook, prayerbook, Bible, and haversack, and some letters to his wife, to be sent to her, and asked me to write and tell her of his death. He was taken to Dr. Murphy's of Woodstock—the home of all Confederates in need.[15]

Hunter heard the news and hastened to Sandie's side. Assisted by Dr. Harvey Black, he dressed the wound. He had the sad task of telling Sandie that the wound was mortal. Hunter offered to stay, even though that meant capture. Sandie refused the offer believing that at such a time of gloom his country could not afford to spare anyone from his post of duty. Dr. McGuire stayed with his friend until midnight. Sandie was conscious, but as the minutes ticked away on the clock, he was filled with more and more pain. He craved ice and was delirious.[16]

The news of Sandie's wound stunned the people of Lexington. Many people came to the Pendleton home to offer their prayers, hopes, and sympathy, and share their mutual woes. General Francis H. Smith of VMI hurried to the rectory and offered his carriage and horses for a trip to Woodstock, expressing the hope that General Early could keep the road open.

Prayers were said in all the churches of Lexington for Sandie's recovery. Dr. William White, Jackson's pastor and a friend of the Pendleton family, called at the home. He knew their sorrow as his son, Hugh, had fallen at Second Manassas.

Sandie's sister, Susan, was filled with grief. "I feel as if we are all so helpless....I can only pray,...'Jesus, Master, have mercy on us'...poor Papa, has been a day of grievous sorrow for him."[17]

Kate, stunned earlier by the deaths of little Janie and of her brother-in-law, Richard, and now nearing the end of her pregnancy, was extremely upset. The doctor gave her medicine and instructed her to be quiet. Kate wrote an unsigned note and tried to send it to General Early hoping he would be able to convey it to her husband.

Early's army was forced back, so Sandie was left at Dr. Murphy's in Woodstock. He lingered and the deathwatch continued. Typical of the war, many of the wounds were untreatable, and there was little to kill the pain. Union doctors offered their help. But nothing could be done. Toward evening on September 22, 1864, just five days before his 24th birthday, Sandie joined Jackson and Boswell, and others, "across the river in a land that is fairer than day." Before he died, he asked messages of love be sent to his family and a lock of his hair to Kate.

Although Lexington is not that far from Woodstock, nearly two weeks passed before the Pendleton family learned of Sandie's death. Conflicting reports kept coming. On October 3, McGuire arrived in Lexington to meet Mrs. Pendleton at the hotel. He told her that he understood that Sandie died on September 23. McGuire had received the message from Dr. Meems[18] who had sent it with a black man coming from Woodstock. The next day a letter from Ned Lee confirmed McGuire's message.

The next morning McGuire talked with Reverend Pendleton and shared all the details of Sandie's wounding, treatment, and final hours. Finally, a letter came from Dr. Murphy on October 17 saying that Sandie had died in his home.[19]

The family was filled with grief, but turned to the Lord for comfort. Later in the month of October, Captain James P. Smith escorted Sandie's body from Woodstock to Lexington, and the young officer was laid to rest near the grave of Stonewall Jackson.

With the victory at Fisher's Hill, Sheridan was able to move at will and started his scorched earth policy, burning the barns and the crops. Sheridan reported to Grant on October 7 from Woodstock that the whole country from the Blue Ridge to the North Mountains had been made untenable for the rebel army. "I have destroyed over 2,000 barns filled with wheat, hay, and farming implements; over seventy mills filled with flour and wheat; have driven in front of the army over 4,000 head of stock, and have filled and issued to the troops not less than 3,000 sheep....A large number of horses have been obtained...."[20]

Sheridan noted that the army had been plagued by bushwhackers, and he was showing little mercy. He also reported that four hundred wagon loads of refugees had been sent from the Harrisonburg area northward to Martinsburg. Most of them were Dunkers and were tired of the war.

The Union cavalry commander concluded by saying, "Tomorrow I will continue the destruction of wheat, forage, etc., down to Fisher's Hill. When this is completed, the Valley, from Winchester up to Staunton, ninety-five miles, will have little in it for man or beast."[21]

>...on every side, from mountain to mountain, the flames from all the barns, mills, grain, and hay stacks, and in very many instances from dwellings too, were blazing skyward, leaving a smoky trail of desolation to mark...and show in a fiery record, that will last as long as war is remembered, that the United States under the government of Satan and Lincoln, sent Phil Sheridan to campaign in the Valley of Virginia.[22]

Confederate General Nathan G. Evans saw a ray of hope. He wrote home telling of a steep climb up the mountain to observe the Union army below. It was "a splendid sight." The Valley Pike looked like a white ribbon in the winter, the country roads like foot paths. The "whole view presented a magnificent natural picture." Nearly every tent of Sheridan's army was visible. What a sight it must have been. Evans was happy. "I believe we can literally rout them if we attack their left flank. Tonight we will probably move....Tomorrow, in all probability, we will have a great battle and I trust a brilliant victory. How many poor fellows must die. How many poor fellows must be maimed for life. How many suffer from wounds. Poor men, poor widows, poor orphans, victims of this bloody work."[23]

Dr. McGuire, who had been treating the wounded from Manassas until this moment, could relate to those statements, and as a doctor he must have wondered, "How long, how long?"

Jed Hotchkiss, with his keen eye for terrain, also believed that there was the possibility of victory with a surprising attack. The enemy must have a weak point. And the scouting report showed that a flank attack had a good chance for success.[24]

As he looked over the situation, Jubal Early met General Ramseur. Earlier, Ramseur had said to General Gordon that he would get his furlough today, a time to go home and see his wife and new baby. Ramseur called to Henry Douglas, "I want to win this battle, for I must see my wife and baby."[25]

Early's initial success was tremendous. He could not have hoped for better results. Middletown might be his Austerlitz.[26] A month ago he had been defeated at Winchester. Now, it looked as though the tide had turned. Gordon cautioned him, saying, "It is very well so far, General, but we still have one more blow to strike."

The tired and hungry soldiers, the rank and file of the command, thought the day had already been won. They stopped to plunder food, clothing, and equipment. Instead of chasing the fleeing enemy, they stopped to eat and to gather shoes. This delay gave Sheridan time to regroup.

Around six o'clock on the morning of October 19, a courier brought the news to Sheridan in Winchester. The previous day, scouts reported Early's camp as being empty, and the message that the Confederates were retiring up the Valley. At first, Sheridan thought it was just a skirmish. He took his time, ate his breakfast, and mounted between eight and nine o'clock. Then he started his famous Winchester ride that made him a great hero.[27]

Three or four miles south of Winchester, he saw the stragglers, wagons, and his retreating army. He ordered guards to stop the retreat, and then standing in the stirrups shouted, "Face about, boys, and follow me."[28] The men cheered, obeyed, turned, and in a few hours stopped the last Confederate offensive in the Shenandoah Valley.

The Union army launched a swift oblique attack on the thinly held Confederate lines. General Gordon's men tried to stem the tide, but they were overwhelmed. From their positions near Belle Grove they gave way and headed for Cedar Creek. Soon others joined in the flight. Discipline gave way. In the midst of it all, General Ramseur received a wound, which he ignored. His horse was shot from under him, but he got another one and rode forth to rally his men. A moment later a bullet entered his right side and tore through both lungs.[29] The young father was carried to the rear, but had to be left in the hands of the victorious Union forces. He was carried to Belle Grove,[30] Sheridan's headquarters, where doctors labored to save him. He knew his wound was fatal, and he faced the end bravely. He realized that he would never see his home, his wife, or his newborn baby.[31]

Sheridan was now in control of the strategic Shenandoah Valley. His campaign can be compared to Sherman's March to the Sea in Georgia. In terms of political and psychological impact, it was just as great. Sheridan's victories in the Shenandoah were a major factor in returning Lincoln to the White House. No longer could the Shenandoah Valley supply Confederate forces or be used as an approach for an invasion of the North.

Congress passed a resolution tendering thanks to "Major-General Philip H. Sheridan, and to the officers and men under his command, for the gallantry, military skill, and courage displayed in the brilliant series of victories achieved by them in the Valley of the Shenandoah, and especially for their services at Cedar Run, on the 19th day of October 1864, which retrieved the fortunes of the day, and thus averted a great disaster."[32] When the news of Sheridan's victory reached Grant at Petersburg, he ordered the cannon to fire a one-hundred-gun salute. Lincoln had found another fighting general. He sent Sheridan this message:

> With great pleasure I tender to you and your brave army the thanks of the nations, and my own personal admiration and gratitude for the month's operations in the Shenandoah Valley, and especially for the splendid work on October 19, 1864.[33]

Shortly thereafter, Sheridan was promoted to the rank of major general in the regular army. The promotion was based on gallantry, military skill, and courage. The citation said that Sheridan reorganized his routed army, averted a disaster, and won a brilliant victory "over the rebels for the third time in pitched battle within thirty days."[34]

Earlier in the war, Jackson had said, "Lose the Valley and Virginia will be lost." And if Virginia was lost, the war would surely be lost. Less than six months after Sheridan gained control of the Shenandoah Valley, the war was over.

The stars over the Valley were obscured by the smoke from barns, crops, and homes burning. Almost every family had lost a loved one from causes related to the war. Most had lost all they held precious. The Civil War has been called "the tragic era." And the fall and winter of 1864–65 certainly was a "tragic era" for the Shenandoah Valley. McGuire suffered through these difficult moments with his friends, comrades, and neighbors. His mother was at home in Winchester; his father, although advanced in years, was on army hospital duty. His brothers were away at war, and his beloved valley was in flames.

# XVI

## "Then Cometh the End"

Hunter McGuire, his mother, and Cornelia McDonald were among those who did not want to give up. But things looked very bleak. Prayers were said for deliverance and for a miracle. "Defeat seemed such a calamity."

One of the few bright spots in dark winter was the wedding of Hugh McGuire, Hunter's brother, and Miss Sally Gallaher in Waynesboro, Virginia. Hugh, six years younger than Hunter, had attended Washington College in Lexington and, therefore, knew Jackson and many members of the Stonewall Brigade prior to the war. At the outbreak of the war, Hugh enlisted in the Rockbridge Artillery and was mustered into Confederate service at Harpers Ferry. For a short time he served as Jackson's military secretary. Then he became a captain in the Ninth Virginia Cavalry. Next, came an assignment with Company E of the Eleventh Virginia Cavalry.

Henry Douglas obtained a furlough to attend the wedding. Henry described the couple.

> The groom was Captain Hugh McGuire, brother of Dr. Hunter McGuire, and a trooper who rode with Rosser. His bride was fair and worthy of him....[1]

Dr. McGuire was one of the groomsmen, along with Douglas and Major General Fitzhugh Lee and four other young officers. The wedding took place in the Gallaher home on January 12, 1865, the service performed by the Reverend W. T. Richardson in the parlor. The celebration lasted until 2:30 A.M. on the thirteenth (from the diary of DeWitt C. Gallaher).

Douglas noted that the bridesmaid he was escorting, Mary Johnson, looked extremely pale. He thought it was nervous excitement or fatigue, but it was far more serious. Mary died within the week and "was buried in the gown and roses she wore at the wedding."[2]

Dr. McGuire remained for several days at the Gallaher home, known as Rose Hall. Troops were encamped on the yard, so there were dances every night. The young people who realized the war was lost, dreaded the spring campaign, but for now "on with the dance."³

On March 1, Captain McGuire returned to the home of his in-laws, reporting that the Yankees were advancing toward Staunton. He had but 150 men to stand against them. These were easily brushed aside by the blue squadrons. Many of McGuire's men were captured. The young captain lost his hat.⁴

General Early arrived with twenty-two hundred infantry and ate breakfast at the Gallaher home. All the civilians in Waynesboro packed up and headed for Charlottesville. Union cavalry galloped by them chasing Confederate troops. It was raining, and the roads were muddy and in terrible condition.⁵

General Sheridan caught up with the remnants of Jubal Early's once proud army. When the action ended, Early's army was finished. During the fighting, the wagon containing McGuire's personal papers and medical records was captured by the Union soldiers. Presumably, they pushed it over a hill and set fire to the contents.⁶ Regardless, McGuire's records and papers ceased to exist as of that moment. In this action, McGuire's records were destroyed. A month later when the big fire swept Richmond, the reports and correspondence to the surgeon general went up in smoke.

Sally Gallaher's brother, DeWitt, escaped into the hills. He looked back and saw a column of smoke. At first he thought it was the family home. Later, he learned that the smoke was from Early's captured wagons that had been set ablaze on a hill near the Gallaher home.⁷

Attempting to avoid the Union pursuers, McGuire tried to jump a fence, but failed. The horse went sprawling. The doctor fell heavily and found himself looking into the muzzle of a Yankee carbine. A Union officer rode up and told the others, "This man is my prisoner. Let him alone." He then took Hunter to the rear and introduced him to Sheridan and his staff. The general was in his tent, surrounded by officers and maps. Sheridan received McGuire cordially and said he was grateful for the release of his doctors on an earlier occasion.⁸ He also told Hunter that he was going to show his appreciation by giving him an immediate release on a two-week parole. Hunter was grateful for this, "but never quite forgave Sheridan for not offering him a drink."

Hunter apparently behaved very well, rather than lashing out at Sheridan for his destruction of the Shenandoah Valley. In gratitude for this treatment, McGuire took the Union officer who had captured him to the home of Mrs. Gallaher,⁹ who fixed them a nice meal. While they were eating, the hostess came to say that Union troops were looting her smokehouse and setting fire to some of her other buildings. The Union officer stopped the soldiers at once. The Union officer was a Lieutenant Vail.¹⁰

McGuire and his captor were both members of the Masonic order. The man in blue had recognized the Masonic sign that Hunter had made when captured and befriended the Mason in gray. While eating at the Gallaher home, Hunter noticed a Masonic picture indicating that Hugh L. Gallaher was also a Mason. The officer in blue was a true fraternal brother, helping one man on the battlefield and protecting the home of another. This was Colonel Forsythe of Sheridan's staff.[11]

Hunter then rode to Staunton to spend his two weeks of parole. He wanted to visit a young lady whom he had met at a wedding. Undoubtedly, this was Miss Mary Stuart. He wrote a note asking permission to visit, and received an invitation to supper. The note from the young lady said, "Don't worry about dress, come as you are."[12] However, at that moment, the only shirt that McGuire had was downstairs being washed.

Little is known of his visit in Staunton. When his two weeks of parole were concluded, McGuire headed east to rejoin what was left of Lee's army.

Hunter's possessions had been destroyed. He had been captured and paroled. Now, misfortune struck his brother Hugh. The young captain had been wounded during the battle of the Wilderness. In early April his cavalry unit skirmished a Union patrol at Amelia Springs. In the action, Hugh received a serious wound. There was little hope for his recovery. Henry Douglas writes, "Generous, gallant, splendid Hugh"[13] had fallen. Painfully wounded, he lingered another month.

On April 2, General Grant finally cracked the Petersburg-Richmond defensive barrier. General Lee was given the news while in church. Throughout the week Lee's depletive army moved westward, still hoping for a miracle.

But it was not to be. There was no food. And Union cavalry and infantry kept coming. At Saylor's Creek, on April 6, Lee lost one-third of his army. Lee thought his forces had been dissolved right there. However, the remainder plodded on to Appomattox, a handful of dwellings, all on one street with a court house and a tavern. With Grant blocking his path, there was nothing for Lee to do but to surrender. After four years of bitter struggle, Lee faced the end, and said, "I'd rather die a thousands deaths."[14]

Lee and Grant met in the home of Wilmer McLean. Lee did not reveal his inner feelings. At first, Grant felt elated, but then when he realized the agony of defeat for his foe, he was saddened. In the parlor on the Palm Sunday in April 9, 1865, the two men drew up terms of surrender.

As Lee rode back to his headquarters, his men flocked around him with tears in their eyes. They could not believe it. They wanted Lee to tell them it was not true.

On the morning of April 12, the remains of Lee's army, led by General John B. Gordon of Georgia, came forth from the Confederate lines. It was a touching moment. Henry Douglas had asked General Gordon "to let my brigade—as it had fired the last shot—the last to stack arms. This he readily granted."[15]

Major General Joshua L. Chamberlain, formerly commander of the Twentieth Maine and one of the most decorated soldiers of the army, was present to receive the surrender. As the brave Confederates drew near, Chamberlain ordered a salute. The men in tattered gray heard the shifting of the arms, quickened their steps, braced their backs, and returned the salute.

Finally, it came time for the men of Henry Douglas to lay down their arms. He tells of the dramatic moment:

As my decimated and ragged band with their bullet torn banner marched to its place, someone in the blue line called for three cheers for the last brigade to surrender. It was taken up...by all those who knew what it meant. But for us this soldierly generosity was more than we could bear. Many of the grizzled veterans wept like women, and my own eyes were as blind as my voice was dumb. Years have passed since then and time mellows memories, and now I almost forget the keen agony of that bitter day when I recall how that line of blue broke its respectful silence to pay such tribute, at Appomattox, to the little line in gray that had fought them to the finish and only surrendered because it was destroyed.[16]

Ann Moss McGuire, the mother of Hunter, Edward, and Hugh, had watched her husband, over 60 years of age, leave to serve as an army doctor at Lexington and Greenswood. Edward served in the U.S. Navy. When the war broke out, however, he joined the Winchester Rifles, but then transferred to the Confederate navy. He served with Lieutenant John Yates Beall in the running of the blockade across the Chesapeake Bay. The home port was in Mathews County, Virginia. Edward was captured and spent a year in a Union prison at Fort Delaware. After his exchange, Edward rejoined Beall and did secret service work for the Confederate government in Canada. Beall was captured, tried as a spy, and hanged at Governor's Island, New York. Edward escaped across the Niagara River. (He returned to Winchester after the war and died in 1882.) And as the war ended, Hugh lay near death from wounds.

Perhaps we can understand Mrs. McGuire's sentiments. Although a devout member of the Episcopal Church in Winchester, she could not bring herself to kneel while prayers were being offered for the president of the United States. She waited until that prayer was completed before kneeling to pray.[17]

# XVII

## Richmond, Virginia

Hunter McGuire took a little time to say good-bye to the men he had known and loved. Like his friend, the deceased Sandie Pendleton, he would be eternally proud to have been a part of Jackson's command. But when he left Appomattox, he departed, like many others, "with just the clothes on his back and the horse between his knees."

McGuire probably stopped briefly at the Gallaher home in Waynesboro, seeking to give comfort to Sally. He may have also stopped in Staunton to visit with Mary Stuart and her family.

Then he continued his ride northward through the devastative acreage of Virginia. He saw again the blackened fields and burned-out barns. And he wept with the family when Hugh died and was buried in what was to become the Stonewall Cemetery[1] at the edge of Winchester. The war had cost dearly.

Hunter rested and tried to regain some of his own strength, as well as assist his grief-stricken parents. Then he learned of a vacancy at the Medical College of Virginia in Richmond. Dr. Charles Bell Gibson had died,[2] and a replacement was being sought. Although probably too young, Hunter applied for the job.

Letters from prominent Virginians were sent on his behalf. Former Governor John Letcher stated, "I take good pleasure in recommending Dr. McGuire." Dr. Robert L. Dabney added, Dr. McGuire is "a brilliant operator, deft surgeon, a man with large experience, a surgical scholar." General Robert E. Lee and Dr. William Nelson Pendleton[3] also wrote, extolling McGuire's abilities. Hunter received the position and borrowed $300 to begin a new life in Richmond.

McGuire must have had many questions as he entered Richmond. The city had been the target of repeated Union attacks, but had withstood all of the attacks until the Confederate lines were broken at Five Forks on April 2, 1865. Then pandemonium broke loose. The citizens grabbed whatever they could carry and fled. Fires were set to destroy military supplies. Soon the flames engulfed tobacco warehouses, railroad bridges as well as the arsenal. The fire raged out of control and burned a large area of Richmond from the James River to Capitol Square.

> Now...as far as the eye could reach, the business portion of the city bordering on the river lay in ruins. Beds of cinders, cellars half filled with bricks and rubbish, broken and blackened walls, impassable streets deluged with debris...such was the scene which extended over thirty squares and parts of other squares.[4]

Hunter gradually developed a medical practice. Most of the patients had no money to pay for his services. Often they brought items of food in trade; however, Dr. McGuire found a strange source of income. The Union officers found occupational duty boring and routine. Often after drinking heavily they engaged in duels, seeking to settle the question of honor. The word leaked that Dr. Hunter McGuire was the best physician, so he was called to treat those who were wounded in the duels. The pay was tremendous, $100 in Union money.[5]

The only hospital in existence was the one managed by the Union-occupied forces. The students of the Virginia Medical College were given clinical instruction in the college's outpatient department. Bedside and operating procedures were taught at the Chimborazo Hospital, courtesy of the U.S. Army Medical Department. Three times a week, McGuire and his students walked the two-mile distance.[6]

As he worked in Richmond, the thoughts of young Dr. McGuire drifted westward to the lovely Shenandoah Valley and to thoughts of Mary Stuart.

Dr. McGuire took about 18 months to establish his practice in Richmond and to get some money in the bank. Hunter McGuire and Mary Stuart were married December 19, 1866, at the Stuart home in Staunton. The Reverend Mr. J. A. Latane, rector of Saint Timothy's Episcopal Church,[7] officiated at the ceremony.

The bride was a lovely woman, "tall and dignified." From the moment of their marriage, she proved to be a worthy mate and a loyal and devoted wife. Mary took interest in all of Hunter's activities. Her advice and constructive criticism proved very helpful. Years later a son remembered one such incident:

> Hunter (she said) I can't understand it; you never see even a dog fight that you don't take sides, and whenever any row in going on you always find that one of the participants is an especially dear patient, or a professional colleague, and you get in the fight as enthusiastically as though it were your own cause. 'It must be the Irish in you.'[8]

Dr. McGuire never attempted to argue the point. He merely smiled, knowing that what Mary said was true.

McGuire also loved horses and always had several good ones in the stable. He was not a good rider, and could poke fun at himself. One of Mary's favorite stories concerned an old lady in Staunton saying to her, "Mary, don't worry, you'll know that sweetheart of yours when he comes down the road, for he and General Jackson are the two worst riders in the army."

Hunter and Mary had nine children. Stuart was born in Staunton on September 16, 1867. Hugh Holmes was next, arriving in Richmond on May 26, 1871. Mary Stuart and the rest of the McGuire children were born in Richmond. Mary was born on December 3, 1872. Fannie Baldwin and Annie Moss, twin sisters, entered the world on December 15, 1875. Another set of twins, Hunter Holmes and Augusta Stuart, were born on May 18, 1878. Margaretta was born on November 24, 1879, and Margaret Cameron, August 13, 1885. Mrs. McGuire was a busy lady. At one time there were five children in the house under the age of five years.[9]

Stuart, as he shared his memories in later years, states, "The children were never allowed to congregate on the front porch for fear passersby might think our house was an orphan asylum. On one occasion when taking her flock to her father's home in Staunton, the conductor of the train, seeing the long procession, said, 'You had better count them, madam.' She was embarrassed because that was the very thing she was doing, and she boarded the train not knowing until she reached Gordonsville whether she had all her children with her."[10]

Part of the summer routine called for Dr. McGuire to travel, and while he was gone, Mrs. McGuire took the children to her home in Staunton or to the country. Her responsibilities were heavy. In addition to the family, there was the management of the servants. There was also a constant stream of visitors to the McGuire house, old veterans, medical colleagues, and others. Mary was an amazing woman, fair and firm with her children. She demanded obedience, and they all respected her to the end of her days.

McGuire had many fine attributes. He was a gifted teacher,[11] preparing his classes well and explaining each step very thoroughly. Many small classes were taught by the bedside of the patient. Some of his methods were those used in the modern training of doctors.

One of his main tasks during the first few years in Richmond was devoted to delivering babies. Almost all births occurred at home and required most of his time.

Much of the surgery was on tumors and bladder stones, with his specialty in abdominal and gynecological operations. In 1868, he made medical history. McGuire operated and bound an abdominal aorta. The only other time this surgery had been performed was in 1817 by Sir Ashley Cooper.

McGuire was in demand at medical meetings as his colleagues wanted to hear him lecture. On one such occasion he was talking to a group of doctors about the use of chloroform. He related that he had administered chloroform to over 40,000 men during the war and never lost a man due to its use.[12]

Dr. William A. Hammond, surgeon general of the U.S. Army, was in the group. McGuire, as humorous as he was temperamental, looked at Dr. Hammond and said he attributed his success with chloroform to the excellent supply that Confederate soldiers captured from Union stores.[13]

In 1881, McGuire resigned his position at the Medical College of Virginia. There were two primary causes: one, friction with other members of the faculty, and two, the size of his own practice. He missed the contact with young doctors so much, that in 1892 he accepted an invitation to assist in the creation of a new medical school in Richmond, to be called the University College of Medicine.

The new school turned to McGuire for guidance, and he was elected president and also served as professor of clinical surgery. The young institution opened with one hundred eighteen students in 1893, and by 1900 had an enrollment of over three hundred. Many were attracted to the school because of the name and stature of Hunter McGuire. "Its early success was due largely to his ability as a teacher, to his wisdom, management and efforts to obtain community support."[14] The curriculum caused other schools in the South to upgrade their medical education. In 1913, the Memorial Hospital, the University College of Medicine, and the Medical College of Virginia merged under the charter of the Medical College of Virginia.

Surgeon Hunter McGuire went to the homes of his patients in Richmond to perform surgery. After the operation he remained with the patient for their care and treatment. The patient was then left in the care of the family. When friends came from out of town for surgery, McGuire made arrangements for them to stay in homes of other friends in Richmond.

McGuire saw the need for some type of hospital facility. In 1877, he enlisted the aid of Annabell Gibson Jenkins, a civic leader in the city. She led a drive that created the Retreat for the Sick,[15] a charity facility. The hospital was established in an older building on Twelfth Street near Marshall Street. The doors were opened on March 14, 1877. Mrs. Jenkins was the manager, but it was open to use by all the doctors.

Things progressed very well for a while. Then, perhaps because McGuire always had more patients than anyone else, he seemed to impose on Mrs. Jenkins. She also took a liking to an intern who one night refused to get up and treat a sick patient, saying if McGuire wanted the person treated, he should come and do it himself. A hearing was held. McGuire, from his military and professional experience, wanted the man dismissed. The board of managers refused the act.[16]

Dr. McGuire immediately moved all his patients from the Retreat for the Sick to local boardinghouses. In 1882, he rented the Richmond House, an old hotel on the corner of Foss and Governor Streets, near the Capitol. On April 19, 1883, St. Luke's Home for the Sick,[17] one of the first private hospitals in the South, was opened. It could accommodate 48 patients who paid $6 to $10 a week for room, board, and care.

St. Luke's Hospital was organized basically the same as the Retreat for the Sick; however, McGuire was the chief doctor. His assistants were Dr. Hugh Taylor and Dr. Lewis.

The hospital consisted of four stories, no elevator. There were 15 bedrooms. "The kitchen, pantry, and storeroom were located in a separated building in the backyard."[18] Unless they were confined to their beds, the patients ate their meals in the first-floor dining room.

Operations were performed in the patients' rooms. A portable table was used. There was no central heat. Each room had its own fireplace. One woman complained of sore feet after a stomach operation, and it was discovered that the operating table had been pushed too close to the fireplace, and the soles of her feet had been burned by the fire.[19]

McGuire quickly saw the need for additional help, as there were no trained nurses at St. Luke's Hospital. The staff, therefore, tried to place a very ill person in a room with someone who was not sick. The one who was moderately ill tried to keep an eye on the other patient.

Five black women with practical nursing experience did the bulk of the work. In 1886, the hospital established a school of nursing. Five young women comprised the class. This was the first school of nursing to be established south of the Mason-Dixon line with the exception of one in New Orleans.[20]

With added help, McGuire was able to pursue one of his goals. He brought a patient into the hospital several days prior to surgery. Having no modern machines for examination, he visited with the patient, listened to their comments,[21] and tried to learn as much as possible about their problem from the nature of the symptoms they shared. If a patient was fearful or had a negative outlook, he postponed the surgery.

While a student in Philadelphia,[22] Hunter noticed that the city doctors had office hours, so he set up office hours in Richmond. The older doctors protested, saying it would not work. He did not set up appointments. But each morning at 8:30, he began seeing patients. A constant flow of persons sought his medical help.

One of the virtues that caused people to come to McGuire was his listening ability. In his counseling and listening he was "like a husband pondering the problems of the sick wife; the father looking down on the affected child."[23] He had his schedule but was a slave of it. When people needed to talk, he listened. Those who knew him said that Dr. McGuire made you feel that you were the most important person in the world.

After seeing and listening to his patients in the morning, McGuire spent the afternoon in house calls. His team of fast horses and red buggy became a Richmond institution. He often made calls until nine o'clock at night. Soon, McGuire had the largest practice in Richmond. Later, after his surgical load increased he was forced to stop making calls unless it was an old friend or a Confederate veteran.

In fact, the only thing that slowed down Dr. McGuire was the visit of "those who had worn the gray." He never turned them away and refused to accept pay for services rendered. He could not be disturbed when they came by his office. Even operations had to wait until he was finished treating or talking with old army friends.

The common, average, ordinary persons also loved him. Treatment was not refused because a person could not pay. When he had office help, many times he would say, "Don't send Mrs. ——— a bill. They've had rough times." He was also instrumental in establishing the Virginia Hospital for the poor of the state."[24]

McGuire saw the need of continuing education for all doctors. It was his desire to have a medical society in each county and in each state. He implored doctors to work together for the good of humanity. His desire was to improve the morale and ability of the doctors not only in the South, but throughout the nation.

He was an advocate of medical meetings, not only for the purpose of socializing, but coming together "to cultivate broad appreciation for each other's work, eliminating all envy of the success of others and to appreciate the work of each other." His goal for those of the medical profession was "lofty aims and united action." Let's show the world we have the stamina of our forefathers."[25] And regarding those who came for treatment, McGuire said, "Make not patients of your friends—but friends of your patients."[26] This philosophy, indeed, summarizes McGuire's life.

Added to his private practice and surgical career was the dimension of writing. Most of this was done late at night after a very demanding day. His literary pursuits fell into three categories:[27]

1. medical reports and journals,
2. addresses and reports to local, state, and national medical groups, and
3. lectures on Jackson and the Civil War.

To him, meetings, writing, and indeed all endeavors should have the goal of helping the physician in his work.

Generous in the gifts of time and money to those in need or those unable to pay, McGuire taught surgery for 15 years at the Medical College of Virginia without compensation. Always believing in helping deserving young students and medical scholarship, McGuire, in 1881, instituted an annual prize for a member of the Medical Society of Virginia for an essay of great merit or research. The amount was $100. In 1897, along with two other doctors, McGuire sponsored an award of $1,000 for a medical history of Virginia.

An evaluation of a person can be seen in the esteem in which he is held by his peers. An evaluation of McGuire's life is seen in the fact that his peers elected McGuire to the following positions:

    1869    President, Richmond Academy of Medicine
    1875    President, Association of Medical Officers of the Army and Navy of the Confederacy
    1881    President, Medical Society of Virginia
    1887    President, American Surgical Association
    1889    President, Southern Surgical and Gynecological Society

Then in 1893 at a meeting in Milwaukee, Wisconsin, Dr. McGuire was elected president of the American Medical Association (AMA). In his inaugural address, Dr. McGuire took one of the most forward-looking positions of his day. In his speech he recommended the establishment of a national department of health. This humanitarian concern, felt by McGuire and others of his day, "stands as a priceless heritage bequeathed by them to all future members of that noble profession."[28]

In his acceptance speech on June 6, 1893, in Milwaukee, Dr. McGuire reviewed some of the achievements of the previous 44 years of the AMA.

He talked about the character of the nation, the advancing prosperity, and power in worldly influence. Hunter said that America "does indeed constitute one of the grand political divisions of earth, and that we represent the most powerful and most progressive nation in the world." And the 100,000 doctors with intelligence, training, skill, and experience were responsible for the "mental and physical emergencies of this entire generation of Americans and the next."[29]

> Gentlemen, we must keep touch and time with all organizations....As patriotic citizens, we owe it to our county, as well as to the Association we represent, earnestly to strive to evolve through hard work, through observation, and knowledge of the needs and demands of all sections of the country, the things that are necessary not only for the preservation of health, but also for the highest conditions of physical and mental development.[30]

This task was in the hands of the doctors representing all sections of the country from Maine to Texas, from California to Virginia.

> Our prime object is the study of disease; the immediate occasion of its outbreak, with the means of preventing it; and the best method of means of loosing its malignant hold, if once fastened upon the community or the individual....
>
> We labor to secure for this organization and for all allied with it, the greatest possible efficiency in the performance of the practical work entrusted to us.
>
> The pagan superstition that disease expressed the anger of the gods of Olympus has disappeared from the human mind.[31]

Nature's laws are orderly and systematized "upon lines that will meet all demands essential to the preservation and maintenance of the universe. When these laws are violated then illness and destruction come. These natural laws of the Creator touch ALL and several of His creations."

A greater life expectancy depends, thought Hunter, upon "a better appreciation and enforcement of hygienic requirement, particularly in terms of water and sewage. The former soldier believed that the nation stood on the threshold of new and exciting discoveries in these fields. However, the united front of the medical profession had to be used to secure the demands for better health.

In statements that seem fitting to every era, McGuire stated, "In order that every obstacle may be removed and every agency brought to bear that can contribute to success, the medical man must gird himself for, a stern battle with ignorance, and prejudice....Inquiry must be pushed in spite of all obstacles."

Water supply, drainage, ventilation, and the proper location of water closets and sinks needed to be checked closely. People needed to be educated as to the standards of good health. He spoke from the benefit of his European travels of the benefit of having boards of health.

The new president of the AMA called for strong local and state medical societies to mingle with other progressive men for "the purpose of interchanging views on current professional topics...and the general welfare of their clientele."

Whenever possible, in counties and cities, societies should be also formed. "In this way...local and general activity will be engendered, and the average standard of professional intelligence raised..."[32]

The *North Carolina Medical Journal* gave its readers a portrait of the new president of the American Medical Association saying:

> He wisely early formed the habit of recording his cases and presenting to the profession...the results of his observations. His contributions to the literature of the profession have been so numerous that it would be impossible to attempt to present a list of them here....
>
> He is in the meridian of life, with the bulk of his best years before him. The profession of the world has reason to look for much more yet from Dr. McGuire.[33]

The same issue carried an article listing the beginning of a new school, College of Physicians and Surgeons, Richmond, Virginia. The charter had been granted in June. "The corporators are many of the best known of business and professional men of Richmond and vicinity." Among them were Dr. Moses Hoge, Judge George Christian, and Dr. Hunter McGuire. "The College will be a three year institution, chiefly on the graded plan, as recommended by the Association of American Medical Colleges, and will in every way strive to take first rank among the prominent colleges of the country.[34] There is also the note, "Dr. Hunter McGuire is President."

Meanwhile, Jefferson Medical College and the University of North Carolina bestowed upon McGuire the honorary doctor of laws degree.

None of the laurels affected Hunter McGuire's outlook on life. Young Stuart was well aware of this. He graduated from the University of Virginia in 1891 and came back to Richmond expecting to get a good job at St. Luke's Hospital with his father. However, one of the black orderlies was ill, and Hunter said to Stuart, "Take his place for awhile." In the months following his job as an orderly, Stuart served as a nurse, janitor, etc., until he filled just about every position in the hospital. "Finally," he says, "I began to see that there was a method in what I had thought was my father's madness. He was teaching me to run the hospital."[35]

# XVIII

## The Summertime of Life

Hunter McGuire's labors in postwar Richmond were productive. He was always interested in people, not necessarily groups, but the individuals. In 1878 he experienced the fulfillment of a lifetime dream, travel abroad. He sailed with his good friend, Dr. Moses D. Hoge,[1] pastor of the Second Presbyterian Church in Richmond. The two had met during the Civil War. Jackson and McGuire attended services at Second Presbyterian on July 13, 1862.[2] During the war, Dr. Hoge ran the naval blockade in an effort to get Bibles and Testaments for the Confederate troops.

After the war, Hoge and McGuire developed a very close friendship. One often stopped at the office of the other. The two men discussed economics, postwar treatment by the North, and referred individuals to one another for spiritual counseling or medical treatment.

Hoge loved to write, as did McGuire. So they kept the citizens of Richmond informed of their travels by sending long letters, which were then printed in the newspapers.

One of McGuire's friends in Dublin, Ireland, was a noted surgeon by the name of George M. Foy. During one of his visits, Foy gave McGuire a complete set of Edward Jenner's original monographs on vaccinations.[3] These had been treasured in Dr. Foy's home, collected at great labor and expense, but he wanted his friend Hunter to have the collection.

The first pamphlet was dated 1798 and dealt with the causes and effects of the vaccination that Jenner discovered in the western counties of England. Several of the pieces bore Jenner's autograph.

After McGuire's death, these were presented to Dr. Sir William Osler in Baltimore. They are now in the McGill Library in Montreal. Osler and McGuire were great friends, and Osler was to serve as an honorary pallbearer.

In 1889, Dr. Foy published a book entitled *Anesthetics Ancient and Modern*. The book was dedicated to his friend Hunter McGuire:

## Chapter 18

TO
HUNTER MCGUIRE, M.D., LL.D.
(RICHMOND, VIRGINIA)
FELLOW AND PAST PRESIDENT OF THE
AMERICAN ASSOCIATION OF SURGEONS,
LATE MEDICAL DIRECTOR OF
THE "STONEWALL" JACKSON CORPS
(2ND) ARMY OF NORTHERN VIRGINIA, C.S.A.
WHOSE NUMEROUS, BRILLIANT, AND
SUCCESSFUL OPERATIONS,
MANY OF WHICH WERE PERFORMED UNDER
GREAT DIFFICULTIES,
HAVE MADE HIS NAME HONORED AND
ESTEEMED IN
TWO HEMISPHERES,
THIS BOOK IS DEDICATED
AS A RESPECT FOR HIS GREAT ABILITIES
AS BOTH A
MILITARY AND CIVIL SURGEON
AND AS A TOKEN ON PERSONAL FRIENDSHIP
BY
THE AUTHOR

Hunter took great interest in the hospitals and medical clinics in London. Likewise, he visited places of historical interest, museums, and art galleries.

He also renewed his friendship with Colonel G. F. R. Henderson[4] of the Royal Army College. Hunter, along with Jed Hotchkiss and others, had supplied the colonel with stories about their life and campaigns with Jackson.

Henderson introduced McGuire to Lord Wolseley, now the commander of Her Majesty's Army, who had visited Jackson's camp at Bunker Hill in the autumn of 1862, and often wrote glowing comments about "Mighty Stonewall." It seems probable that McGuire and the English officer had met in 1862.

This led to a great privilege. On September 11, 1896, Hunter McGuire, the doctor from the little town of Winchester and a man whose highest rank was that of major, was invited to be with General Garnet Wolseley to review 35,000 English troops. Only one thing detracted from the experience. Dr. McGuire had not ridden a horse in years, and for the next several days, he was very sore and stiff.[5]

Henderson and Wolseley were very much impressed with the Virginia physician. The British commander was very happy to talk with McGuire about the greatest man he ever knew, Robert E. Lee.

On September 26, 1896, Wolseley wrote to McGuire asking, "Do you possess a letter written by General Lee that you could give to an admirer of the greatest soldier in the second half of this century."[6] For the English leader, the fame of Lee was increasing "constantly."

On November 3, Henderson wrote to McGuire in gratitude for his visit, saying, "I never spent two more pleasanter days than I did with you listening to stories about Jackson and his soldiers."[7]

Henderson had been designated by General Wolseley to write about Jackson and the American Civil War. From time to time, Henderson sent his manuscript to McGuire and to Jed Hotchkiss for their evaluation. Letters crossed the Atlantic leading to a book that has become a classic, *Stonewall Jackson* and the *American Civil War,* by Colonel G. F. R. Henderson.

After the publication of the book, Henderson and McGuire continued their correspondence. Occasionally, the English officer wrote asking McGuire for materials for his files. One request was for a list of all the staff officers who had served with Jackson.

McGuire was in great demand for patriotic and civic addresses. Undoubtedly, his greatest address was given at the dedication of the Jackson Memorial Hall at the Virginia Military Institute in Lexington, June 23, 1897. As he faced the crowd that day, McGuire said, "The noblest heritage I shall hand down to my children is the fact, that Stonewall Jackson condescended to hold me and treat me as his friend."[8]

McGuire would have done well as an orator or politician. He spoke in flowery language and compared Jackson with King Arthur, Alexander the Great, and Constantine. He noted that within the past two hundred years the English-speaking peoples had produced but five "soldiers of the first rank—Marlborough, Washington, Wellington, Robert Lee, and Stonewall Jackson."

> I have heard them declare (military students) that Jackson's campaign in the Shenandoah Valley...was the finest specimen of strategy and tactics of which the world has any record; that in this series of marches and battles there was never a blunder committed by Jackson; that this campaign in the Valley was superior to either of those made by Napoleon in Italy...Another British soldier told me that for its numbers the Army of Northern Virginia had more force than any other army that ever existed.[9]

The physician-orator praised his native state as he talked about the five great soldiers by saying, "Three were born in the State of Virginia;...two of them lie, side by side, here in Lexington...the three consecrating in death the soil of Virginia, as in life, they stamped their mother State as the native home of men who, living as they lived, shall be fit to go on quest for the Holy Grail.[10]

McGuire then listed the qualifications for the honor, relating what he and others had seen in the quiet of camp and in the rush of battle. The doctor accepted the traits as listed by Lord Wolseley.

First, the power, the instinct to "divine the condition and the purpose of your enemy..." Second, the strategy and tactics devised that are most likely to defeat the purpose of the enemy. Third, the "physical and moral courage—the absolute self-reliance—that takes the risk of decision, and the skill that promptly and properly delivers the blow that shatters the hostile plans." The fourth item was that the calm judgment that cannot be shaken in emergency, or coolness under fire. And the fifth, and perhaps the most important in some eyes, "the provision—the caution—that cares for the lives and well being of the private soldiers, and the personal magnetism that rouses the enthusiasm "and affection, that makes the commander's presence on the battlefield the incentive to all the human beings can dare."[11]

McGuire related the many times, in two years of war, that Jackson looked at the enemy, his commanding opponent, sized up the situation, and struck. McGuire considered this to be a rare gift of Jackson's.

In fact, the one loss that Jackson sustained at Kernstown was a time when he relied on the opinions of others instead of trusting his own judgment and instinct.

In the eyes of Dr. McGuire, Jackson was "always calm and self-controlled." He never lost his balance for one moment.

The doctor gave an illustration of Jackson's care for his troops. Headed for Second Manassas without a supply train, he sent two officers with a squad of cavalry ahead of the army to tell people he was coming, requesting provisions for his hungry men. "The people responded nobly to this appeal and brought liberal supplies of flour and meat and other things to the troops."

In discussing personal magnetism, McGuire asked a series of questions.

> Did he arouse the enthusiasm of his men? What army ever had more unbounded confidence in its general, than did the army of Jackson? And what general ever trusted and depended on his army more than Jackson? Jackson knew the value of the Southern volunteer better and sooner (as I believe) than any other of our great leaders...Did his men love him? What need of proof or illustration? Do we not feel it today in every throb of our hearts, though the long years have rolled away...
> 
> Although Jackson was kind and true, his views on war were stern. War means fighting; to fight is the duty of a soldier, march swiftly, strike the foe with all your strength and take away from him everything you can. Injure him in every possible way, and do it quickly....[12]

McGuire concluded his speech in Lexington by saying that Caesar spent eight years in winning his first series of victories. Napoleon's career spanned 20 years, and Hannibal about 15 years. "No other great commander in the world's history has in so short a time won so great a fame as Jackson.

> And so I leave the grave of my General and my friend, knowing that for centuries men will come to Lexington as to a Mecca, and to this grave as to a shrine, and wonderingly talk of this man and his mighty deeds. I know that time will only add to his great fame. I know that his name will be honored and revered forever, just as I know that the beautiful river flowing nearby, will sing an unceasing requiem to his memory—just as I know that the proud mountains, like the vast chain of sentinels, will keep eternal watch over his honored grave.[13]

Reading the speech in detail, one sees the friendship between Jackson and McGuire. In fact, it was said of the physician, "Owing to his habits of observation, his excellent memory, and his close association with Jackson, there is perhaps no

# The Summertime of Life

other man living who has more vivid impressions of the great soldier than Dr. Hunter McGuire, or is better prepared to talk upon his phases of character."[14]

Among the many notes of praise coming to McGuire for his address in Lexington was one from England, from Colonel Henderson.

Mary and Hunter McGuire were busy in 1896–1897, helping to establish a Confederate museum. Colonel Henderson wrote, saying, he thought the three books that Jackson carried in his haversack would be a great addition to the museum. The books were Jackson's *Bible, Napoleon's Axioms,* and *Webster's Dictionary.*

Dr. McGuire was also active in the behalf of veterans. After the Civil War, the Union veterans formed the Grand Army of the Republic, the forerunner of the American Legion. Those who had served in the South organized the United Confederate Veterans (UCV). Among the purposes were these items:

> …to cheer one another in cordial comradeship…to remember fallen comrades, and bury their dead, and succor the old and dependent, and care for the widow and the orphan.[15]

Although the Grand Army of the Republic and the United Confederate Veterans had not thought of continuing a useless strife or of fanning the fires of sectional animosities, there was a problem that the Confederate veterans wished to see corrected.

Soon after the war, books were published covering the Civil War. Many of these were used in the schools of the land. Most of them were printed in the North due to conditions in the desolate South. In these books, the South was made to look like a villain, and the aggressor in the war. Southern aims were falsified and some of their leaders defamed.

In August of 1897, Dr. McGuire was vacationing at Bar Harbor, Maine. During the month, he met an old friend, Captain John Cussons of Glen Allen, Virginia.[16] Cussons was also a Confederate veteran. He had made a study of the histories being used in Northern schools and was upset with their slanted views. As they talked, McGuire and Cussons decided to take steps to set the record straight.

In the autumn of 1897, there was a large meeting of concerned citizens and veterans. The presiding officer was Dr. McGuire, and Cussons made a stirring speech. This took place at the Lee Camp of the UCV in Richmond, Virginia. McGuire was made chairman of the History Committee. The committee selected a list of books that presented, in their eyes, an untrue story of the Civil War. Systematically, each controversial point in the black-listed books was refuted. The committee's aim was to refute the teaching that slavery was the main cause of the war and to dismiss the books of the dozen writers.

The introduction to the list reads:

> When the thin ranks of the armies of the Southern Confederacy were at last dissolved, the survivors of the great struggle, who had marched and fought so long and well, went back across untilled fields and to impoverished homes. Whatever perils they had faced, and whatever losses had suffered, they had not lost their manhood, and they had not surrendered their self-respect and honor, nor anything of their faith in the right and

justice of their cause. With a heroism as true and honorable as that displayed on many fields of battle, they returned to work, without capital and almost without implements, some of them crippled for life, and some in broken health, but unscathed in honor and uncrippled in will. They were again to prove their manhood on more difficult fields; to feed and reclothe their women and children, to rebuild their homes and to reestablish government and all the institutions of their civilization.[17]

A generation was growing up with mistaken ideas about the war, and the Southern cause, however, right or wrong, was being made to look dishonorable. "The youth of the whole South were being stealthily robbed of a heritage glorious in itself and elevating and ennobling to themselves and all who came after them. It was a condition and a process which could not be consented to for a moment. There was no surrender at Appomattox, and no withdrawal from the field which committed our people and their children to a heritage of shame and dishonor. Jefferson Davis and Robert E. Lee were not traitors. The desire of the committee was that the threatening evil on the doorstep of every school be met and corrected.

Dr. McGuire states that he knew Lee and Jackson were both opposed to slavery. This was a matter of public record. They did not fight to preserve the institution of slavery. They were Virginians, however, fighting to preserve states' rights.[18]

McGuire also remarked that being a part of the famed Stonewall Brigade, he knew not one man in thirty who owned a slave. "The South fighting for the money value of the negro! What a cheap and wicked falsehood."[19]

The History Committee compiled a list of books they wished to be banned, and another list which contained the names of the books that were fair and just in their treatment of the conflict.

Dr. McGuire devoted himself to this work the same as he did to the care of the soldiers of the Army of Northern Virginia and in the hospital work in Richmond. "I intend...to vindicate the South from the oft-repeated charge that we were the aggressors in bringing on the war....This will be my last labor of love for the dear Southern people."[20]

Later in the report, statements were made concerning the conduct of the war, based primarily on Union sources. Sherman's March to the Sea and Sheridan's wanton destruction in the Shenandoah Valley were contrasted against Lee's regard for private property and the protection of civilians.

The committee certainly had strong evidence in this field, including letters and orders from President Lincoln, Secretary of War Stanton, and Union generals. All one has to do is to read Sherman and Sheridan's reports, and the destruction and suffering of the civilians can be readily seen.

Letters were introduced from Union soldiers in which they wrote home and laughed about burning homes and the slaughter of animals and made derogatory remarks about the Negroes.

Some Union soldiers lamented, "The wanton destruction of property....There was no restraint....The country was left to become a howling waste."

*The Summertime of Life*

The discipline of the Southern army speaks for itself. It must have been extremely difficult when in Pennsylvania in the summer of 1863 to refrain from plundering. Many were Virginians and their farms and villages had suffered very badly. Even Henry Kyd Douglas, McGuire's friend, when he saw what happened to his home in Maryland after Antietam, wanted to go North and burn and teach the Yankees a lesson.

In the Maryland campaign of 1862, two things amazed the natives as Lee's army marched through: their dirty, ragged condition, and their discipline, even though without food and rations.

When General John McCausland burned Chambersburg in the summer of 1864, Lee wrote:

> The commanding general considers that no greater disgrace could befall the army, and through it to our whole people, than the perpetration of the barbarous outrages upon the innocent and defenseless and the wanton destruction of private property, that have marked the enemy in our country...It must be remembered that we make war only on armed men, and that we cannot take vengeance for the wrongs our people have suffered without lowering ourselves in the eyes of all whose abhorrence has been excited by the atrocities of our enemy, and offending Him to whom vengeance belongeth, without whose favor and support our efforts must all prove in vain.[21]

Officers from Austria, Prussia, and England expressed great surprise to members of the committee "that volunteer troops, proved by nearly twenty-seven months of unparalleled ruthlessness and wantonness, of which their country has been the scene, should be under such control, and should be willing to act in harmony...with President Davis and General Lee."[22]

Perhaps the best summary of the work chaired by Dr. McGuire is found in the words of the committee:

> We...feel that we owe it to ourselves and to the memories of those who suffered and died for the cause we fought so hard to maintain, to let our children know the truth as to the causes of the conflict, and how it was conducted.[23]

The result of the work of Hunter McGuire and George L. Christian was *The Confederate Cause and Conduct in the War Between the States*. This was published in Richmond in 1907. Dr. McGuire worked on this during the evening of March 18, 1900.

During the postwar years in Richmond, many officers and men from the Army of Northern Virginia came to see Dr. McGuire. James P. Smith was frequently in Richmond, traveling from his parish in Fredericksburg to edit "The Central Presbyterian." Henry Heth, the general whose command opened and closed the Gettysburg campaign, enjoyed the moments he spent with McGuire.

Close ties remained with Jed Hotchkiss, Jackson's mapmaker. McGuire and Jed wrote often. Jed had been successful in teaching, mining, and journalism, and was very active in the Presbyterian Church of Staunton.

# Chapter 18

In the autumn of 1898, Hotchkiss, now 70 years old, had to make a business trip, and the only train available was a freight engine. The jolting was too much for the elderly gentlemen. He was ill when he returned home. The local doctors could not help him. Jed went to St. Luke's Hospital in Richmond, and McGuire removed a kidney stone. By the end of December, he was back home in Staunton and able to attend the Christmas services at his church. Jed lived another 13 months, dying on January 17, 1899.

Speaking at the Lee-Jackson dinner, McGuire said of Hotchkiss, "I would like…to pay my simple, loving heartfelt tribute to the last one who has just crossed over the river, brave, noble, and faithful Jed Hotchkiss."[24]

# At the Confederate Capitol

Monday, March 19, 1900, started as a routine day for McGuire. While riding from his downtown office to St. Luke's Hospital he became ill. Although he lost his speech, he was still able to make the driver realize that he wanted to return home.[1]

Mary McGuire immediately summoned other physicians. When they arrived, Hunter was at his desk, with his head buried in his hands. Tears were running down his cheeks. He tapped the left side of his head with his finger, thus diagnosing his own case. The problem was an embolism of the brain causing him to lose his speech and bringing paralysis to his right hand and leg.

The family moved to their country home at Westwood.[2] Eventually, Hunter was able to walk, but he never regained his speech. Death came on Wednesday, September 19, at 10 A.M. The Richmond Academy of Medicine in its memorial resolution stated: "God endowed him with great natural gifts of head and heart and great opportunities came into his life. He had power to comprehend and adopt them to the needs of every occasion. He has left his stamp on this community, on us as a local profession, and on the professional world. Tenderly we treasure his memory; deeply we mourn his loss."[3]

Dr. George Ross, the chairman of the group, stated:

> Hunter McGuire, the gifted surgeon is dead...he was the most brilliant luminary in the medical constellation of the South. His name is part and parcel of American surgical history. It is the synonym for accuracy in the surgical diagnosis and skill in surgical technique...His personality was most charming...he won all hearts by his simplicity...At various times in his life he was a professor in three medical colleges, and died serving one...His strong personality and wide reputation were the most potential factors in the upbuilding of the University College of Medicine to its present conspicuous position. No teacher more instructive or more pleasing ever lectured to a class, and no man ever more genuinely enjoyed the affection

and confidence of his pupils…His generosity was limited only by the opportunities for dispensing it. His hand was always ready to do service for the poor and needy…He was gifted with rare executive ability and an irresistible personal magnetism…He measured up to every responsibility laid upon him, from the morning of life until the shadows of life's evening fell suddenly upon him…He began his career in this community after he had heard the requiem march sounding the death-knell of the Southern Confederacy on the field of Appomattox, and from the first day that he sought to serve this people until the day when he was driven to his own door, speechless, stricken with paralysis in his buggy,…there was no let up in his work….[4]

Services for Dr. McGuire were held on September 21 at St. Paul's Episcopal Church in Richmond. At the stroke of noon, Bishop Robert A. Gibson opened the service.[5] He was assisted by the Reverend Preston Nash and the Reverend James Power Smith. Smith had escorted the bodies of Jackson and Pendleton to Lexington. Now he was in a service for Hunter McGuire.

Every seat in the church was filled, and the chancel was banked with floral tributes. Members of the Richmond medical profession served as active pallbearers. The list of honorary bearers was extremely long. Among them were Reverend Beverly Tucker Lacy, the minister who often shared in services at the bivouacs of Jackson's Corps; Judge George L. Christian, the man who assisted McGuire to prepare a true history of the Confederate cause; his traveling companion to Europe, Dr. M. D. Hoge, Jr.; and General Fitzhugh Lee.

Student nurses came dressed in their white uniforms, along with many Confederate veterans, members of the faculty, students from the medical school, and others from civic groups in Richmond, and of course, the families and others who had been touched so deeply by the life and efforts of Dr. McGuire.

Lilies of the valley were placed on the steps leading to the altar of St. Paul's. Their fragrance filled the air. The choir sang, "Just as I am," and "Rock of Ages."[6] A quiet peace filled the sanctuary.

After the impressive Episcopal services, the procession moved to Hollywood Cemetery where Hunter Holmes McGuire was laid to rest "under the shade of the trees," taking his place with the great and small from Virginia.

An editorial in the *Richmond News* stated that McGuire was one of the most striking personalities known to the current generation of Virginians. Few men were as much respected for their professional and patriotic opinions. "It may be doubted whether anybody has lived in Virginia since Lee and Jackson died who was loved by more people."[7]

His character was strong, straightforward, yet modest and down-to-earth. He was a man of courage, always ready to speak the truth, and always ready to counsel a friend. He was held in great esteem by Lee, Jackson, and Lord Wolseley. Yet, he was as tender as a woman[8] and expressed regret when his medical skill could not help his patients. "A more absolutely true and loving friend never lived upon this earth."

In the obituary carried in the *Journal of the American Medical Association*, it was noted that Dr. McGuire "has been a leading figure in American medicine for the last thirty or forty years....In his state and throughout the South generally he was a leader in his profession, and there were few who had a record that so endeared them to their fellow citizens....In his death his country has lost one of the foremost members of our profession."[9]

Shortly after Dr. McGuire's death, a memorial association was formed with the purpose of erecting a suitable monument honoring the public and professional services of the doctor in gray, and the friend of all Virginians.

Contributions came to the association not only from Richmond and a portion of the Commonwealth of Virginia, but from all over the South and even from Northern friends. Most of the contributions were small, coming from the poor people to whom he had given a helping hand, a friendly smile, and a note of hope.

William Cowper was selected to design the monument, and the Virginia legislature enacted special legislation granting permission to locate the monument in Capitol Square near that of Stonewall Jackson. Now the task was complete, and on this first Thursday in 1904 the dedication and unveiling took place.

About 1 P.M. drums of the approaching troops could be heard. Soon the head of the column appeared, and to lively music the troops walked down the avenue.

Nearing the stands constructed for the dedication, the band began to play "Maryland, My Maryland," and then one of Jackson's favorites, "Dixie." Behind the troops came the veterans from the Lee and Pickett camps of the United Confederate Veterans. Following the old soldiers were members of the faculties and students from the two medical colleges, so closely associated with the life of Hunter McGuire.

The *Richmond Times-Dispatch* reported:

> In the presence of a distinguished company of Virginians and amid the roar of cannon and the blare of bands, there was unveiled in the historic Capitol Square of Richmond yesterday a noble and enduring memorial in bronze to HUNTER HOLMES McGUIRE, the South's great surgeon and one of her most eminent and illustrious sons.[10]

Thousands were in attendance. Four governors of Virginia were present, along with scores of legislators, lawyers, doctors, and citizens. They were gathered to pay tribute to "one whose service had been equally to both—to the bleeding soldier upon the field and to the helpless pleading sufferer in the time of peace."[11]

The *Richmond Times-Dispatch* continued its coverage by saying:

> It was upon hallowed ground that the assemblage stood, and the influence of the environment had been never before so keenly felt. To one side stood the gray and venerable Capitol, around which cling the traditions of the Commonwealth; to the other arose the new and massive city hall, in striking contrast to the former. A short distance to the rear the mansion of the governor of the state could be seen through a bower of trees; almost on a parallel with it, at the other end, arose the spire of St.

Paul's Church, where Davis, the Confederate chieftain, sat when Lee's appalling message urging evacuation was placed in his hands. All around were leafless trees and sloping avenues, half hiding the cold, bronze forms of the enshrined. Jackson, from his stony pedestal, arose a few feet from the still form of him who, on the battlefield and in the camp, had been his friend and advisor; Washington, from his towering height, was the center of a mute gathering of warriors and statesmen, not far off; from the other side, Henry Clay gazed with changeless eyes far over the historic hills of Chesterfield.[12]

When the bands reached Capitol Hill, the crowd became quiet. Dr. James Power Smith, McGuire's friend, rose to offer prayer.

> We thank Thee for the gift of strong men, wise and brave and faithful...
>
> We thank Thee for the blessed Healing Art, and for that profession which has given us so many who have blessed their generation by their genius and skill, and their sympathy for the troubled and suffering. Unto one of them we have built a monument...We have placed it here, that his name may long be remembered, and that his memory may abide for the good of the city and his native Commonwealth, which he loved so ardently, and to which he gave so much of the devotion and power of his life...
>
> Let Thy favor ever abide upon the institutions to which he gave so much of his life and strength; upon his comrades, the men of the gray; upon the home he loved so dearly, and upon the Commonwealth of Virginia....[13]

The Honorable George L. Christian then made the presentation address, noting, "We are assembled today...to unveil and to donate to Virginia a monument to one of her most eminent, devoted, and patriotic sons."

Christian introduced his speech by talking of the fame and success of Stonewall Jackson. This led to his remarks that McGuire was assigned a part "by one of the greatest leaders of that drama of the war." He stated that McGuire more than fulfilled the hopes and expectations of Stonewall; therefore, his name will be forever linked with the fame of Jackson.

> It is, therefore, fitting that the friend and companion of the great "Stonewall," the man who shared his tent and his mess in the days of his trials and his triumphs, who at the same time enjoyed his friendship and his confidence, and to whom he assigned great and important trusts for execution, should have his statue placed near that of his illustrious and incomparable chieftain.
>
> But not only did Dr. McGuire win such fame as should entitle him to this statue by his great services as the Medical Director of the Second Corps of the immortal Army of Northern Virginia, but he rendered even greater services and won even greater fame after the war was over. It was then amid the desolations left by that conflict of our ruined land; to relieve the sufferings and the sorrows of our stricken people, and to keep the history of their deeds, and of the principles for which they fought, right and true.[14]

Christian continued:

> By the authority of the General Assembly of Virginia, this statue is placed on these grounds, along with those of so many others of her sons who have won fame in Virginia's service, and whom she delights so much to honor. On behalf, and in the name of the Hunter McGuire Monument Association, I am commissioned to present this monument to Virginia....[15]

Governor Montague accepted the gift as an evidence of McGuire's "rich contribution to science." He also noted that the monument will "proclaim with duration and eloquence of bronze the memories of a patriot, soldier, and scientist, whose life powerfully impressed his day and generation."

Now it was time for the main address. The featured speaker was Major Holmes Conrad of Winchester, "one of the most brilliant speakers of the country." He spoke of the traits of McGuire, which had grown through the years and gained him the love and confidence of his country.

Dr. Conrad noted that McGuire's character was built on strength and stability. Naturally there were many references to Jackson. Hunter McGuire was always the trusted friend and close companion of his chief. Conrad's closing words were:

> He loved the South, her people and her interests, and gave thought and labor to their advancement. He loved with a love that knew no bounds, Virginia, and her people, his brethren of her soil. These were the objects of his deep solicitude, and upon them were the final labors of his life.[16]

Now it was time for the big moment, the unveiling of the statue. Little Hunter McGuire, the eight-year-old grandson of the great doctor, pulled the cord unveiling the monument. Tears dimmed the eyes of family members as they saw the profound likeness of their loved one. "The statue throbbed with life."

Again the bands played "Dixie," and "Maryland, My Maryland." Thirteen guns fired a salute. The crowd cheered. After the official ceremonies, many lingered to talk and share memories of Dr. McGuire. There he was, etched in stone, in the heart of Richmond, seated in a chair, just like he had been so many times when people from all walks of life had come to him for treatment and advice. Many walked up to the monument to read the inscription.

TO
HUNTER HOLMES MCGUIRE, M.D., LL.D.
PRESIDENT OF THE AMERICAN MEDICAL
AND OF THE
AMERICAN SURGICAL ASSOCIATIONS:
FOUNDER OF THE UNIVERSITY COLLEGE OF MEDICINE:
MEDICAL DIRECTOR, JACKSON'S CORPS
ARMY OF NORTHERN VIRGINIA:
AN EMINENT CIVIL AND MILITARY SURGEON
AND BELOVED PHYSICIAN.
AN ABLE TEACHER AND VIGOROUS WRITER;
A USEFUL CITIZEN AND BROAD HUMANITARIAN;
GIFTED IN MIND AND GENEROUS IN HEART,
THIS MONUMENT IS ERECTED BY HIS MANY
FRIENDS.

# Chapter 19

The state of Virginia, Stonewall Jackson, the Confederacy, medicine, people, around these revolved the life of Hunter Holmes McGuire, physician, humanitarian, teacher, and good Samaritan.

Now from his monument Dr. Hunter McGuire looks over his beloved Richmond. Nearby is the Medical College of Virginia. He sits calm and dignified, almost like listening to the cries of the human heart. Perhaps, he is counseling or just listening like a good country doctor. Perhaps, he is thinking of Winchester, the Shenandoah Valley, or his experiences with "Mighty Stonewall." Hunter Holmes McGuire, a teacher, surgeon, humanitarian, a Virginian, and Southerner has taken his place in history.

# A Continuing Legacy

Not only has Dr. Hunter McGuire been enshrined on the grounds of the capitol, but several miles from the Virginia Medical College, there is a continuing legacy to his professional skill and compassion.

In 1982, St. Luke's Hospital observed its 100th anniversary. Hunter McGuire started the original St. Luke's—named after Luke, the physician, and the writer of the Gospel—at the corner of Ross and Governor Streets (near the capitol). Then a new St. Luke's, the most modern of its time, was constructed at the corner of Harrison and Grace Streets in 1899.

Hunter McGuire did not live to see the success of this fine, new facility. However, his son Stuart, a member of the staff, continued the work begun by his father.

Stuart McGuire was a frail child and suffered from a spinal disease all his life. This, however, did not stop him from serving others or from continuing the work of his father.

Graduating from the Virginia Medical School in 1891, Stuart went to work with his dad. And "under his father's guidance was taught every aspect of hospital management." When Hunter McGuire died, Stuart inherited the work. Thus today, St. Luke's has a family heritage, the McGuire family contributions.[1]

With the outbreak of World War I, Stuart was called to military service. He was ordered to France and became chief surgeon of Base Hospital, No. 45. One of his assistants was a pretty, young nurse from St. Luke's by the name of Ruth Robertson. She was young "with beautiful blue eyes and a softly modulated voice."

Arriving in the United States from Ontario, Canada, Ruth had made her way to Richmond and to St. Luke's. There, she became a nursing supervisor, and then crossed the ocean to assist in the ministry to the wounded. Soon she became chief nurse of the military hospital in France. Shortly after their return from Europe, Stuart McGuire and Ruth Robertson were married. The wedding occurred at the Robertson home in Walkerton, Ontario, on August 12, 1919. Returning to Richmond, the young couple reopened St. Luke's.

# Chapter 20

In 1923, Stuart organized the McGuire Clinic. "This concept of a selected group of physicians working together was the first for their part of the country."[2] The McGuire Clinic is still functioning near the new St. Luke's Hospital and is a part of the continuing legacy of the McGuire family.

Stuart continued his medical practice and the administration of St. Luke's until 1930. His health started to fail and "he gradually relinquished his work."[3] By 1941, he had become an invalid, but he maintained his keen interest in the hospital. Often, board meetings were held in his bedroom. Stuart presided over these sessions, propped up in bed.[4] He died in 1948.

> There was a special feeling about the St. Luke's on Grace Street. To native Richmonders, the mere mention of the name brought to mind numerous things—its location, a favorite physician, a nursing graduate, a family member's illness or some special event, hospital connected, which had played a role in their lives.[5]

In 1971, Humana, Inc., "a national investor-owned hospital company from Louisville, Kentucky," acquired St. Luke's. Four years later in 1975, a new modern St. Luke's Hospital opened on Parham Road. It is

> equipped with the latest in medical technology and equipment. It is a 200-bed medical and surgical hospital...offering full body scanning, ultra sound and nuclear medicine, neurology/neurosurgery, orthopedics, oncology, physical therapy,... (and many other medical services).[6]

Likewise, the School of Nursing, established by Dr. McGuire, continues to produce "graduates of highest quality. It is one tradition which has been handed down through the years."

St. Luke's is accredited by the Joint Commission on the Accreditation of Hospitals. It remains dedicated to the philosophy and goals of its founder, Dr. Hunter Holmes McGuire, to "providing compassionate care along with the best medical treatment possible for its patients."[7]

The new hospital cost $10 million and is five stories in height. Dr. John P. Lynch, of the McGuire Clinic, was the master of ceremonies at the dedication service. Music was provided by the United States Marine Band of Quantico, Virginia. The main speaker was Hugh Downs, a well-known journalist and television personality. Several descendants of the famed Dr. McGuire were present for the gala occasion.[8]

Two letters received during the 100th anniversary of St. Luke's in 1982 speak for themselves. From the governor's mansion:

> Please accept my warmest congratulations on the occasion of the Centennial Birthday of St. Luke's Hospital. The outstanding accomplishments of your hospital in medical care—and in behalf of the community you reach—stand as a superb example to all those who are familiar with the rich history of the hospital. The hospital has been a leader in training medical personnel and was renowned as the first school of nursing in Virginia, and is credited with medical advancements critical to the mark of

# A Continuing Legacy

progress in modern health care. I salute the hospital also for continuing in the pioneering spirit of its great founder, Dr. Hunter Holmes McGuire, one of the truly outstanding figures in the history of American medicine....

*Charles S. Robb*
Governor

From 1600 Pennsylvania Avenue in Washington came this letter:

I am pleased to send greetings to all who celebrate the one hundredth anniversary of the founding of St. Luke's Hospital.

The efforts you have made to improve services, to train medical personnel, to further medical advancements, and to adopt high standards of health care have enriched the quality of life throughout the Old Dominion. You have helped the most vulnerable among us.

I send my congratulations and best wishes for another century of skilled and compassionate health care.

*Ronald Reagan*

In St. Luke's Hospital and the School of Nursing, the state of Virginia, the South, and the nation have "the continuing legacy" of "the pioneering spirit of its great founder, Dr. Hunter Holmes McGuire."

Dr. Stuart McGuire continued the work of his father at St. Luke's. And even in 1983, another Dr. Hunter McGuire, the grandson of Jackson's surgeon, continued as chief of surgery at the McGuire Veterans Hospital in Richmond. In buildings, health care, and descendants, the compassionate work of Dr. Hunter Holmes McGuire reaches out as a "continuing legacy."

# Notes

## I—WINCHESTER, VIRGINIA

1. For histories of Winchester, and Frederick County, consult T. K. Cartmell, *History of Frederick County, Virginia* (Winchester, 1909); Frederic Morton, *The Story of Winchester in Virginia* (Strasburg, 1925); Garland R. Quarles, *The Streets of Winchester* (Winchester, 1958). The Virginia Room in the Handley Library, Winchester, contains a wealth of local material.
2. Stuart McGuire, M.D., Hunter Holmes McGuire, M.D., LL.D., in *Annals of Medical History*, vol. 10 (January 1938). Cited hereafter as Stuart McGuire, *Annals*. Stuart McGuire was Hunter's son. William Stanard, *The McGuire Family in Virginia* (Richmond, 1926).
3. Stanard, p. 33.
4. William P. McGuire, "Winchester Medical College," in the *Virginia Medical Monthly*, 1924.
5. The Cooke family was prominent in Shenandoah Valley medical and literary circles. Dr. John Esteen Cooke, 1783–1853, was a part of the McGuire school, and then a professor in Kentucky. See Francis R. Packard, *History of Medicine in the United States*, vol. 2 (New York, 1931), pp. 780–82.

## II—HUNTER HOLMES McGUIRE

1. Stanard, p. 108.
2. Ibid., p. 103.
3. Ibid.
4. Stuart McGuire, *Annals*, p. 3.
5. Ibid., p. 5.
6. Ibid., p. 6.

## III—SPARKS

1. Bruce Catton, *The Coming Fury* (New York, 1961). This is an excellent book detailing the events that ignited the Civil War.
2. The *Winchester Virginian*.
3. Jackson, Lee, and others realized early in the war the strategic importance of the Shenandoah Valley. Later, Grant and Sheridan saw it, and the devastation of the Valley helped to bring an end to the war.
4. Beverly M. Munford, *Virginia's Attitude toward Slavery and Succession* (Richmond, 1909), p. 282.

## Notes to Pages 6–12

5. Cornelia Peake McDonald, *A Diary With Reminiscences of the War and Refugee Life in the Shenandoah Valley, 1860–1865* (Nashville, Tenn., 1934), pp. 14–15.
6. Ibid. Her book describes the life of the residents of Winchester, McGuire's hometown, during the war.
7. The Virginia legislature met in secret on April 17, 1861. However, they voted to leave the Union, but delayed the announcement until militia troops could converge on Harpers Ferry.
8. MacDonald, p. 16. See James L. Robertson, *The Stonewall Brigade* (Baton Rouge, La., 1963).

### IV—HARPERS FERRY, VIRGINIA

1. John Imboden, "Jackson at Harpers Ferry in 1891," *Battles and Leaders of the Civil War* (New York, 1884–1887), vol. 1, pp. 111–16. See also, Robertson, pp. 3–4.
2. Imboden, p. 113, and Robertson, p. 9.
3. Joseph E. Johnston graduated from West Point with the Class of 1829. He was wounded five times in the Mexican War and cited for bravery on three occasions. In April of 1861 he was named a major general of Virginia forces, and a brigadier general in the Confederacy. He was then assigned to command Harpers Ferry. He led skillfully at First Manassas. A feud with Jefferson Davis kept him from using his talent to the fullest.
4. The Twenty-seventh Regiment of Virginia was comprised mostly of young men from Lexington and the western counties of Virginia.
5. William Nelson Pendleton was a graduate of West Point, Class of 1831. After serving several routine tours of army duty, he resigned to enter the ministry of the Episcopal Church. He moved from All Saints Church in Frederick, Maryland, in 1854, and served the church in Lexington until his death. During the early days of the war, he commanded the Rockbridge Artillery. He was the father of Alexander Swift "Sandie" Pendleton, a young man who became one of McGuire's best friends.
6. William G. Bean, *The Liberty Hall Volunteers* (Charlottesville, 1964). This unit came from Washington College, taking their name from the old hall on the campus. The lads were incorporated into the Fourth Virginia Infantry. Many of them were studying for the Christian ministry.
7. For more information on the Rockbridge Artillery, see William T. Poague, *Gunner with Stonewall* (Jackson, Tenn., 1957).
8. Robertson, p. 10.
9. Stuart McGuire, *Annals*, p. 35.
10. Stuart McGuire, *Annals*, p. 7; Hunter McGuire, General Thomas J. Jackson, in the *Southern Historical Society Papers*, vol. 19 (Richmond, 1891), p. 301. Cited hereafter as *SHSP*.
11. W. F. Bean, *Stonewall's Man, Sandie Pendleton* (Chapel Hill, N.C., 1959). Young Pendleton became a member of Jackson's staff on June 25, 1861. He and McGuire soon became very close friends.
12. Henry Kyd Douglas, *I Rode with Stonewall* (Chapel Hill, N.C., 1940). See Douglas Papers, Bast Museum, Boonsboro, Maryland.
13. Dennis Frye, *The Second Virginia Infantry* (Lynchburg, Va., 1984). This book is a part of the Virginia regimental series. It has excellent material on Hunter McGuire's regiment.

### V—CONFEDERATE MEDICAL SERVICE

1. Francis T. Miller, *Photographic History of the Civil War*, vol. 7 (New York, 1911), p. 238.
2. Ibid., p. 239.
3. Ibid., p. 240.
4. Ibid., p. 244.
5. Ibid., p. 246.
6. Ibid., p. 250.
7. Ibid., p. 248.

8. For more information see *The War of the Rebellion—The Medical and Surgical History of the War of the Rebellion* (Washington, D.C., 1875–1888). Six volumes: three volumes on medicine, three on surgery.
9. Richard T. Hutchinson, Jonathan Letterman, 1824–1872. "A Paper Prepared for the General Reference and Historical Unit of the U.S. Army Medical Service, June 1965," p. 2.
10. Letterman was born in Canonsburg, Pa., December 11, 1824. He went to Jefferson College and Jefferson Medical School. From 1849–1861 he practiced medicine with the U.S. Army on the frontier. In June 1862 he was appointed medical director for the Army of the Potomac. Mr. Hutchinson says "So basic was his contribution to military medicine the world over, that it remains today, modified, but essentially unaltered from the way he formulated it over one hundred years ago," from page 1 in the staff paper.
11. Leo Riordan, "Battlefield Medicine," a historical writing for Jefferson Medical School, p. 11.
12. Miller, vol. 7, p. 237; Bell I. Wiley and Hirst D. Milhollen, *They Who Fought Here* (New York, 1959), p. 210. Cited hereafter as Wiley.
13. Ibid., p. 238.

## VI—BATTLE OF FIRST MANASSAS

1. Falling Waters is a small community just south of the Potomac River, located in what is now West Virginia. Here Jackson and what was to become the Stonewall Brigade had their baptism of fire in July of 1861.
2. Susan P. Lee, ed., *Memoirs of William Nelson Pendleton* (Philadelphia, Pa., 1893), p. 146. The Pendleton Papers are located at the University of North Carolina.
3. McDonald, p. 17.
4. U.S. War Department, comp., *War of the Rebellion: A Compilation of the Official Records of the Union and Confederate Armies*, vol. 2 (Washington, D.C., 1880–1891), p. 157. Cited hereafter as *O.R.*
5. John O. Casler, *Four Years in the Stonewall Brigade* (Girard, Kansas), p. 21.
6. Robert L. Dabney, *The Life and Campaigns of Lieut. General Thomas J. Jackson* (New York, 1866), p. 212. Dabney, a Presbyterian clergyman, served on Jackson's staff during part of 1862. He was the first biographer of Jackson, getting some of his material from McGuire.
7. Hunter McGuire, *Southern Historical Society Papers*, vol. 19 (Richmond, Va., 1881, 1891), p. 309. Cited hereafter as *SHSP*.
8. Ibid., p. 304.
9. Ibid., p. 306.
10. Idem.
11. Ibid., p. 303.
12. Ibid., p. 304.
13. Jackson's Report of First Manassas, *O.R.*, vol. 2, pt. 1, p. 485.
14. Wiley, p. 210.
15. Casler, p. 40.

## VII—BRIGADE SURGEON

1. Wiley, p. 210.
2. Ibid., p. 211.
3. Ibid., p. 212.
4. Ibid., p. 213.
5. William M. Owen, *A History of the Washington Artillery* (Boston, 1885), p. 130.
6. Allan Nevins, ed., *A Diary of the Civil War, 1860–1865, George T. Strong* (New York, 1962), p. 261.

# Notes to Pages 21–29

7. Ibid.
8. Ibid., p. 213.
9. Two excellent chapters on the medical problems of the soldiers, and the complexities of medical treatment were written by Bell I. Wiley. See "The Depths of Suffering," in *The Life of Billy Yank* (New York, 1952), pp. 124–51, and "The Deadliest Foe," in *The Life of Johnny Reb* (New York, 1971), pp. 244–69.
10. Bell Wiley, *The Life of Johnny Reb*, p. 250.
11. Diary of William Bradley, April 25, 1865.
12. Diary of W. C. McClellan Bradley, April 25, 1865.
13. Letter from Thomas Warrick to Martha Warrick, March 22, 1863, Alabama Archives.
14. Theodore Gerrish and John S. Hutchinson, *The Blue and the Gray* (Bangor, Maine, 1884), p. 180.
15. Wiley, *The Life of Johnny Reb*, p. 215.
16. Ibid., p. 220.
17. Ibid., p. 221.
18. Ibid.
19. Ibid.
20. *Medical and Surgical History of the War of the Rebellion*, surgical vol. 1, pt. 3, p. 902.
21. Ibid.
22. Wiley, *The Life of Johnny Reb*, p. 230.
23. Ibid., p. 232.
24. J. K. F. Mansfield, commanding the Union XII Corps, was shot in the stomach at Antietam and removed from the field in the manner described.
25. Wiley, *The Life of Johnny Reb*, p. 232. Dr. James Oliver notes on Antietam.
26. These comments were made many times by the wounded.
27. *Medical and Surgical History of the War of the Rebellion*, surgical vol. 2, pt. 3, p. 902.
28. From a listing of the items a surgeon should have available.
29. Confederate surgeons carried the rank of major.
30. Jackson admonished McGuire to wear his green sash when he rode into Winchester to visit his mother in March of 1862.
31. Wiley, *The Life of Johnny Reb*, p. 225.
32. Ibid.
33. Ibid.
34. See the report of Jonathan Letterman in the selection of Antietam Hospitals.
35. U.S. Army Military Medicine pamphlet, Fort Detrick, Maryland.
36. W. W. Keen, "Military Surgery in 1861–1918," *Annals of the American Academy of Political and Social Science,* 80 (1918), pp. 14–15.
37. Wiley, *The Life of Johnny Reb*, p. 230.

## VIII—BACK TO WINCHESTER

1. Mary Anna Jackson, *Memoirs of Stonewall Jackson* (Louisville, Ky., 1895), p. 204.
2. Col. G.F.R. Henderson, *Stonewall Jackson at the American Civil War*, vol. 1 (New York, 1898), p. 160.
3. Henry K. Douglas, *I Rode with Stonewall* (Chapel Hill, N.C., 1940), pp. 15–16.
4. James Langhorne to his mother, November 12, 1861, Virginia Historical Society, Richmond.
5. M. A. Jackson, p. 203.
6. Jackson to his wife, Winchester, November 16, 1861.

7. A noted hotel in the heart of downtown Winchester, once owned by the McGuire family, now a department store.
8. Casler, p. 73.
9. Milo Quaife, ed., *Alphesus Williams: Letters from the Cannon's Mouth* (Detroit, 1959), p. 59. Contains the letters of General Williams to his daughters back home.
10. Douglas, p. 20.
11. Ibid.
12. M. A. Jackson, p. 236.
13. M. A. Jackson speaks of staying at the Grahams, and her husband visiting them in May of 1862, and November of 1862. Some of the Graham-Jackson correspondence is included in the book. Pages 485–507 comprise Dr. Graham's recollections of Stonewall Jackson.
14. Ibid., p. 212.
15. Ibid., pp. 241–42.

## IX—THE VALLEY CAMPAIGN

1. John Worsham, *One of Jackson's Foot Cavalry* (New York, 1912), p. 68. Additional materials on this campaign, which Dr. McGuire considered Jackson's best, can be found in Robert G. Tanner, *Stonewall in the Valley* (New York, 1976), and the biographies of Jackson by Dabney, Henderson, and Vandiver.
2. M. A. Jackson, pp. 246–47.
3. Stuart McGuire, *Annals*, p. 13.
4. Ibid.
5. The Jedediah Hotchkiss Papers, the Library of Congress. See also Archie P. McDonald, ed., *Make Me a Map of the Valley: The Civil War Journal of Jackson's Topographer* (Dallas, 1973).
6. Hotchkiss Papers, Journal, March 26, 1862.
7. Ibid., April 14, 1862.
8. Ibid., March 27, 1862.
9. Rude's Hill is between Mount Jackson and New Market. This provided a good defensive position.
10. One of Jackson's axioms, perhaps adopted from his readings of Napoleon and his tactics.
11. Jackson was impressed with the beauty of the Valley from the time of his arrival in November of 1861. He stated that to his wife and to Douglas.
12. Hotchkiss Papers, Journal, Mary 23, 1862; Dabney, p. 373.
13. Tanner, p. 23. Hotchkiss Journal for May 24, 1862, describes the captured supplies.
14. Douglas, p. 59.
15. McGuire's report of captured items.
16. *O.R.*, vol. 22, pt. 1, pp. 707, 720–24.
17. Stuart McGuire, *Annals*, p. 9.
18. E. D. Newton, "The Red Cross Society: Its Origin and Its First Practical Adoption" (New Orleans, April 25, 1906).
19. George H. Weaver, *Bulletin of the Society of Medical History of Chicago* (January 1933); Philip Adolphus, in the *Medical and Surgical History of the War of the Rebellion*, a note on McGuire releasing the captive doctors.
20. Hunter McGuire, *SHSP*, p. 315.
21. Ibid.
22. Robertson, p. 40.
23. McGuire, *SHSP*, p. 314.
24. Stuart McGuire, *Annals*, p. 13.

# Notes to Pages 41–61

25. Speech of Hunter McGuire at the dedication of Jackson Hall at VMI.
26. Interview with the McGuire family.

## X—THE SUMMER OF 1862

1. Stapleton Crutchfield, Jackson's chief of artillery in 1862, was a graduate of VMI. He lost a leg at the Battle of Chancellorsville. He served later in the defense of Richmond and was killed at Sayler's Creek in April of 1865, just a few days prior to the end of the war.
2. Douglas, p. 98.
3. Hunter McGuire, *SHSP*, p. 305.
4. Bean, *Pendleton*, p. 73.
5. Moses D. Hoge was the pastor of the Second Presbyterian Church in Richmond. He preached to the troops after the Seven Days, and McGuire and Jackson attended his church. Hoge ran the blockade to bring Bibles and tracts from Europe. After the war, Hoge and McGuire became very close friends and traveled to Europe together.
6. Hunter McGuire, *SHSP*, p. 313.
7. Ibid., p. 305. In August of 1862, Mrs. Jackson wrote to Hunter McGuire and urged him to get Jackson to spare himself. Letter, McGuire Collection, University of Virginia.
8. Jackson's comments of his visit to Second Presbyterian, July 13, 1862.
9. Willie Preston was the young son of Colonel J. T. L. Preston and Maggie Junkin Preston. Maggie had been Jackon's former sister-in-law. Jackson had been thinking of placing young Preston on his staff. He wrote a very touching letter of sympathy to the parents.
10. Hunter McGuire, *SHSP*, p. 305.
11. *O.R.*, *Medical and Surgical History*, vol. 2, pt. 3, case no. 447.
12. Ibid.
13. Hunter McGuire, *SHSP*, p. 313.

## XI—SHARPSBURG AND BUNKER HILL

1. Letter from Robert E. Lee to Jefferson Davis, September 3, 1862.
2. John Divine and others, *Loudoun County in The Civil War* (Leesburg, 1861), p. 41.
3. J. G. Hamilton, ed., *The Papers of Randolph P. Shotwell*, vol. 1 (Raleigh, N.C., 1929), p. 310.
4. Hotchkiss Papers, Journal, September 5, 1862.
5. Heros Von Borcke, *Memoirs of the Confederate War for Independence*, vol. 1 (New York, 1931), p. 185.
6. *Battles and Leaders*, vol. 1, p. 238.
7. Douglas, p. 148.
8. Best's Grove was between modern-day U.S. 355, the road to Urbana, and the Buckeystown Pike. It was near the present Francis Scott Key Mall in Frederick, Md.
9. Pendleton had served All Saints Episcopal Church from 1846–1854, when he moved from Frederick, Maryland to Lexington, Virginia.
10. James P. Smith, "With Stonewall Jackson," *Southern Historical Society Papers*, vol. 5 (Richmond, 1920), p. 16.
11. Douglas, p. 150.
12. Letter from Jackson to his wife, September 8, 1862.
13. Hunter McGuire, *SHSP*, vol. 10, p. 511.
14. Douglas, p. 153.
15. Letter from Jackson to Lee, September 15, 1862.
16. Owen, p. 139.
17. Henderson, p. 234.

18. The Smith farm, where Jackson had his headquarters, still stands at the west end of Sharpsburg, Md. It was here that McGuire worked throughout the seventeenth of September. Douglas, p. 174.
19. McGuire often related this account of Antietam during his Jackson lectures.
20. Douglas S. Freeman, *Lee's Lieutenants*, vol. 2 (New York, 1945), p. 398.
21. Hill, *O.R.*, vol. 19, pt. 1, p. 981.
22. Freeman, vol. 2, p. 224.
23. James Longstreet in *Photographic History of the War*, vol. 2, p. 76.
24. Francis W. Palfrey, *The Antietam and Fredericksburg* (New York, 1882), p. 126.
25. R. L. Walker in *Battles and Leaders*, vol. 2, p. 681.
26. Henderson, p. 262.
27. Shepherdstown, on the original route into the Shenandoah Valley, was settled by Thomas Shepherd and others. See Mary Bedinger Mitchell in *Battles and Leaders*, vol. 11, p. 689.
28. Ibid.
29. Ibid.
30. Ibid.
31. Ibid.
32. *Hagerstown Torch and Herald*, September 24, 1862.
33. Jonathan Letterman's Report, *O.R.*, vol. 19, pt. 1, p. 107.
34. Walker in *Battles and Leaders*, vol. 2, p. 682.
35. Letterman, *O.R.*, vol. 19, pt. 1, p. 159.
36. Letter from Sandie Pendleton to Nancy Pendleton, October 26, 1862.
37. Letter from Jackson to his wife.
38. Ben Ritter, "Jackson's First War-time Portrait, The Widow's Favorite," *Civil War Times Illustrated* (February 1979), pp. 37–39. See Douglas, p. 199.
39. McDonald, notes on November 16, 1862.
40. The Graham notes in the Jackson papers.
41. Douglas, p. 197.
42. Stuart McGuire, *Annals*, p. 14.

## XII—FREDERICKSBURG AND MOSS NECK

1. Letter from Sandie Pendleton to his mother, November 28, 1862.
2. McDonald, December 4, 1862.
3. Ibid.
4. Hotchkiss Papers, Journal, December 13, 1862.
5. Letter from William Nelson Pendleton to his wife, December 15, 1862.
6. Douglas, p. 203.
7. Hunter McGuire, *SHSP*, p. 309.
8. Hotchkiss Papers, Journal, December 16, 1862.
9. Douglas, p. 207; Roberta Corbin Kinsolving, "Stonewall Jackson in Winter Quarters; Memories of Moss Neck in the Winter of 1862," *Confederate Veteran* 20, p. 24. Cited hereafter as Kinsolving.
10. Ibid.
11. Douglas, p. 208.
12. Ibid., p. 210.
13. Letter from Sandie Pendleton to Mary Pendleton, December 28, 1862.
14. Douglas, pp. 207, 214.

## Notes to Pages 72–86

15. Letter from Sandie Pendleton to his mother, December 31, 1862.
16. Letter from Sandie Pendleton to Mary Pendleton, December 28, 1862.
17. Ibid.
18. Ibid.
19. Hotchkiss Papers, Journal, January 19, 1863.
20. Letter from Kate Corbin to Sally Munford, February 17, 1863.
21. Ibid., February 21, 1863.
22. James Keith Boswell Diary, February 25, 1863.
23. Hotchkiss Papers, Journal, March 8, 1863.
24. Hunter McGuire's speech at Lexington, June 1897.
25. There were two Yerby homes near Hamilton's Crossing. The largest was "Belvoir." It was here that General Maxcy Gregg died and Lee recovered from his late March heart attack. And this is where Jackson stayed. Information supplied by Robert Krick, chief historian of the Fredericksburg-Spotsylvania National Battlefield.
26. Boswell Diary, March 16, 1863.
27. Letter from Sandie Pendleton to Mary Pendleton, March 19, 1863; Letter from Kate Corbin to Sally Munford, March 28, 1863.
28. Jackson, p. 396; Douglas Diary, March 17, 1863.
29. Letter from Sandie Pendleton to Kate Corbin, March 26, 1864.
30. M. A. Jackson, p. 408; J. P. Smith, "With Stonewall Jackson," *SHSP*, vol. 5 (Richmond, 1920), p. 44.
31. Smith, *SHSP*, vol. 5, p. 50.
32. McDonald, p. 135.

### XIII—CHANCELLORSVILLE

1. J. P. Smith, p. 46.
2. Ibid.
3. Ibid., p. 53.
4. See Hunter McGuire's account of the wounding of Jackson.
5. The date is wrong on the original copy. It should be Monday, May 4, 1863.
6. Hunter McGuire, "The Wounding and Death of Stonewall Jackson," *Richmond Medical Journal* (May 1866). The classic McGuire description of this sad event.
7. Note from Sandie Pendleton to the governor of Virginia, May 10, 1863.
8. For detailed accounts of the final tribute in Richmond, see the writings of Douglas, Mrs. Jackson, and the Pendleton Papers.
9. Douglas, p. 229.
10. Ibid., p. 230.
11. Ibid.
12. McDonald, p. 161.
13. Ibid., p. 162.

### XIV—WITH GENERAL RICHARD S. EWELL

1. Richard S. Ewell was a graduate of West Point, Class of 1841. He served in the Mexican War and with the regular army prior to the Civil War. He resigned in 1861 to receive a commission in the Confederate army. He rose in rank to major general and lost a leg at Groveton, Virginia. Hunter McGuire performed the surgery. See Percy Hamilin, *Old Bald Head* (Strasburg, Va., 1940). Ewell had just been married when he assumed command of the Second Corps in the spring of 1863.

2. General Orders No. 411, calling for the chaplains to hold services of thanksgiving for the victory of Second Winchester.
3. Douglas, p. 243.
4. Sandie Pendleton to Kate Corbin, June 25, 1863. The Second Corps was across the Potomac and was at Greencastle, heading for Chambersburg and Carlisle.
5. McDonald, p. 157.
6. Ibid., p. 161. She states that she saw Dr. McGuire in Winchester.
7. Ibid., p. 162.
8. Sandie Pendleton to his mother, June 25, 1863, from headquarters, two miles north of Chambersburg in a grove of trees.
9. Ibid., June 18, 1863.
10. James W. Sullivan, *Boyhood Memories of the Civil War, 1861–1865* (Carlisle, 1933), pp. 20–21.
11. Sandie Pendleton to Kate Corbin from Carlisle Barracks, June 29, 1863. The flag was that of the Thirty-second North Carolina.
12. Ibid., June 28, 1863. Once again McGuire displayed his Irish temper.
13. Sullivan, p. 23.
14. Hotchkiss Papers, Journal, June 29, 1863.
15. Douglas, p. 247.
16. Ibid., p. 252.
17. John Imboden, "The Confederate Retreat," *Battles and Leaders of the Civil War*, vol. 3, pp. 420–21.
18. McDonald, pp. 177–78.
19. Ibid., p. 179.
20. Bean, *Stonewall's Man*, p. 148. Letter from Sandie Pendleton to his mother, August 27, 1863.
21. Hotchkiss Papers, Journal, November 14, 1863.
22. *Richmond Daily Enquirer*, November 23, 1863.
23. Letter from Sandie Pendleton to Kate Corbin, November 25, 1863.
24. Ibid.
25. Ibid.
26. Letter from Kate Corbin to Sally Munford, November 29, 1863.
27. Letter from Sandie Pendleton to his father, December 4, 1863.
28. Letter from Mrs. Pendleton to Susan, January 3, 1864, Pendleton Papers.
29. Letter from Sandie Pendleton to Kate Corbin, Morton Hall, April 15, 1864.

## XV—THE YEAR OF 1864

1. Jubal A. Early (November 3, 1816–March 2, 1894) was born in Franklin County, Virginia. Graduating from West Point in 1837, Early served briefly with the military and then resigned to practice law. In 1841, he was elected to the state legislature. When the war began, he became colonel of the Twenty-fourth Virginia Infantry. Rising to the command of the Second Corps, he returned to a law practice in Lynchburg after the war. However, in the interim, he advocated a new Confederacy, and was bitter toward the Union.
2. The death of Colonel Willis was described to his father, Dr. F. J. Willis of Savannah, Georgia, in a letter from Sandie Pendleton, sent on May 31, 1864. See the Hunter McGuire Papers, Alderman Library, University of Virginia.
3. Ibid.
4. Douglas, p. 292. By this time Douglas had recovered from his wound and had been released as a prisoner of war.
5. Hotchkiss Papers, Journal, July 2, 1864.
6. Frederick County, Maryland Historical Society Records, Frederick, Maryland.

## Notes to Pages 97–106

7. Ransom note in possession of Frederick County government.
8. Lewis Wallace, the Union commander on the banks of the Monocacy, wrote the famous novel *Ben Hur*. See also Glenn H. Worthington, *Fighting for Time* (Frederick, 1934).
9. The William Allan Papers, *Southern Historical Society Papers*, Southern Historical Collection, University of North Carolina, Chapel Hill. Colonel Allan was from Winchester and was chief ordnance officer of the Second Corps. Allan's book *Stonewall Jackson's Campaign in the Shenandoah Valley of Virginia* (London, 1912), is an excellent source of Jackson study. After the war, Allan became headmaster of the McDonogh Boys School near Baltimore. He was survived by his wife, Elizabeth Preston Allan, of Lexington, Virginia.
10. Letter from Stephen Dodson Ramseur to his wife, August 29, 1864.
11. Ibid., September 11, 1864.
12. Robert Emmett Rodes (March 29, 1829–September 19, 1864) was born in Lynchburg and graduated from VMI. After graduation he remained as an instructor. In 1851, he resigned to become a civil engineer. Entering the Civil War as a colonel of the Fifth Alabama Infantry, he proved a capable officer and was soon given brigade command. He was made a major general for gallantry and leadership at Chancellorsville.
13. George E. Pond, *The Shenandoah in 1864* (New York, 1883), p. 171.
14. Ibid., p. 172.
15. Douglas, pp. 312–13. See Bean, *Pendleton*, p. 210.
16. Susan Lee, p. 372.
17. Susan Lee to her husband, September 25, 1864. The Pendleton Papers, *Southern Historical Society Papers*, Chapel Hill, N.C.
18. Ibid., October 4, 1864.
19. Letter from A. E. Pendleton to her husband, October 18, 1864.
20. Sheridan's Report, *O.R.*, vol. 43, pt. 1, pp. 30–31.
21. Ibid.
22. Pond, p. 172.
23. Clement A. Evans, ed., *Confederate Military History*, 12 vols. (Atlanta, Ga., 1899).
24. Hotchkiss Journal, October 17–18, 1864.
25. Douglas, p. 317.
26. Freeman, vol. 3, p. 584.
27. Thomas Buchanan Read "*Sheridan's Ride*." Inspired by his ride from Winchester to rally his troops and turn a Confederate victory into an overwhelming defeat, this poem made Sheridan a popular hero in the North, and became a part of the classical literature of the war.
28. Philip H. Sheridan, *Personal Memoirs of Philip H. Sheridan* (New York), pp. 66–68.
29. Douglas, p. 317.
30. Belle Grove, one of the early manor houses in the Valley, became Sheridan's headquarters.
31. Stephen D. Ramseur, attended by physicians of both armies, died far from home on October 20, 1864. He had been the youngest West Pointer in the Confederacy to become a major general.
32. The Congress of the United States, February 9, 1865.
33. Letter from President Lincoln to General Sheridan, October 22, 1864.
34. War Department, promotion to major general (Sheridan), November 8, 1864.

### XVI—"THEN COMETH THE END"

1. Douglas, p. 323.
2. Ibid., p. 324.
3. DeWitt Clinton Gallaher, *A Diary Depicting the Experiences of Dewitt Clinton Gallaher in the War Between the States...* (Charleston, W.Va., 1945). According to this diary the wedding was held January 12, 1865.

4. Ibid., March 1, 1865.
5. Gallaher Diary, March 2, 1865.
6. See also Hotchkiss Diary for March 2, 1865.
7. Gallaher Diary, March 2, 1865.
8. Ibid.
9. Ibid.
10. Ibid.
11. Ibid.
12. Stuart McGuire, *Annals*, p. 11.
13. Douglas, p. 324.
14. See Freeman, *Lee's Lieutenants*, vol. 3, p. 712, and following. This is the account of the final chapter of the Army of Northern Virginia at Appomattox.
15. Douglas, p. 344.
16. Joshua Chamberlain, *Passing of the Armies* (New York, 1915), p. 265.
17. Stuart McGuire, *Annals*, pp. 13–14.

## XVII—RICHMOND, VIRGINIA

1. The Stonewall Cemetery was established on the east side of Winchester, along the Berryville Pike. It was a part of the third Battle of Winchester, which marked the beginning of the end for Jubal Early's Confederate army. The cemetery was dedicated on June 6, 1866, the anniversary of the death of Turner Ashby. Hugh McGuire is buried in the cemetery, along with young men from the South who fell in the fighting around Winchester, Kernstown, Fisher's Hill, and Cedar Creek.
2. Stuart McGuire, *SHSP*, p. 139.
3. Dr. Pendleton had become close to Hunter McGuire through the friendship of his son Sandie.
4. Trowbridge, *The Desolate South*, p. 84.
5. Stuart McGuire, *SHSP*, p. 140.
6. Ibid., p. 141.
7. Alexander Hugh Holmes Stuart.
8. Stuart McGuire, "Memories of My Father and Mother," p. 43.
9. The Official Records of St. Timothy's Episcopal Church, Staunton, Virginia.
10. Stuart McGuire, p. 43.
11. Ibid.
12. Ibid.
13. Ibid., p. 44.
14. Ibid., p. 149.
15. Hunter McGuire, speech at a national medical meeting.
16. Ibid.
17. Dr. George Ross in a tribute at the Richmond Academy of Medicine, September 20, 1900.
18. Stuart McGuire, *Annals*, p. 20.
19. Ibid.
20. Ibid.
21. Ibid., p. 21.
22. Ibid.
23. Ibid.
24. Ibid., p. 25.
25. Ibid., p. 26.
26. Ibid.

## Notes to Pages 114–123

27. Ibid., p. 31.
28. Stuart McGuire, *Annals*, p. 31.
29. Ibid.
30. Ibid; Address to the AMA in Milwaukee, Wisconsin, June 1893.
31. Ibid.
32. Ibid., p. 154.
33. Ibid.; *Journal of the American Medical Association*, June 1893.
34. Stuart McGuire, *Annals*, p. 15
35. Idem.

### XVIII—THE SUMMERTIME OF LIFE

1. Dr. Moses Drury Hoge (September 17, 1819–January 6, 1899) was a member of a prominent Presbyterian family. His father had been founder of the Union Theological Seminary in Virginia. Hoge was an ardent Southerner, and a frequent preacher in the camps of Jackson's command. He took the fall of Richmond and the Confederate defeat very badly. Dr. Hoge officiated at the wedding of Jackson's daughter. See John W. Schildt, *Jackson and the Preachers* (Parsons, W.Va., 1982).
2. Stuart McGuire, *Annals*, p. 23. Second Presbyterian Church records.
3. Ibid., p. 23.
4. Colonel G.F.R. Henderson had been an instructor at Sandhurst, the English equivalent of West Point. He was assigned the task of writing a biography of Jackson's life by Lieutenant General Wolseley, the British officer who had visited Jackson's camp at Bunker Hill in the autumn of 1862.
5. Stuart McGuire, *Annals*, p. 23.
6. The McGuire Collection, University of Virginia.
7. Henderson to McGuire, *Annals*, November 3, 1896.
8. Hunter McGuire, speech at the dedication of the Jackson Memorial Hall, Lexington, Va., June 23, 1897. Full text among the Hotchkiss Papers, Library of Congress.
9. Ibid.
10. Ibid.
11. Ibid.
12. Ibid.
13. Ibid.
14. *Richmond-Dispatch*, July 19, 1891. The editor introducing an article prior to the unveiling of the Jackson statue in Lexington.
15. George L. Christian and Hunter McGuire, *The Confederate Cause and Conduct in the War Between the States* (Richmond, 1907).
16. From the founding papers of the United Confederate Veterans, setting forth the purposes of their existence.
17. John Cussons emigrated from England at age 16 for America. He worked for the *Free Press* of Detroit, and then went to live with the Sioux Indians, studying their mode of living. During the war he served with Hood's Confederate command and was captured. He is buried in Richmond's Hollywood Cemetery.
18. From the discussions, meetings, and writings which led to *The Confederate Cause and Conduct in the War Between the States*.
19. The result of the research by Cussons and McGuire was *The Confederate Cause and Conduct in the War Between the States*.
20. From the Introduction to *The Confederate Cause and Conduct*.
21. Cussons and McGuire, p. 18.
22. Ibid., p. 23

23. Ibid., p. 25
24. Hunter McGuire, Speech in Richmond, January 20, 1899.

## XIX—AT THE CONFEDERATE CAPITOL

1. Stuart McGuire, *SHSP*, p. 158.
2. Ibid.
3. The Richmond Academy of Medicine and Surgery Resolution, September 20, 1900.
4. Ibid. Statement by Dr. George Ross, chairman of the Resolutions Committee.
5. Stuart McGuire, *SHSP*, p. 158.
6. Ibid.
7. Ibid., p. 159.
8. Ibid., p. 29.
9. *Journal of the American Medical Association*, September 29, 1900.
10. *Richmond Times-Dispatch*, September 20, 1900.
11. Stuart McGuire, *SHSP*, vol. 1, p. 253.
12. Ibid.
13. Ibid., p. 252.
14. Ibid.
15. Ibid.
16. Ibid., p. 254.

## XX—A CONTINUING LEGACY

1. Materials for this chapter come from "St. Luke's Hospital," supplement to *Richmond Times Dispatch*, Sunday, August 10, 1975; and "St. Luke's Hospital, A Century of Care and Caring, 1882–1982." Courtesy of the McGuire Clinic, begun by Dr. Stuart McGuire and submitted by Dr. John Lynch, past director of the McGuire Clinic. *Richmond Times Dispatch*, Sunday, October 17, 1982.
2. *Richmond Times-Dispatch*, October 17, 1982, p. 7.
3. Ibid., August 10, 1975, p. 6.
4. Ibid.
5. Ibid., p. 3.
6. *Richmond Times-Dispatch*, August 10, 1975, p. 3.
7. Ibid., October 17, 1982, p. 3.
8. Ibid.

# Bibliography

## PRIMARY SOURCES

Alexander Robinson Boteler Papers. Duke University Library. Durham, N.C.

DeWitt Clinton Gallaher Diary.

*Hagerstown Torch and Herald.*

Hunter McGuire Papers. Alderman Library. University of Virginia, Charlottesville.

Hunter H. McGuire Papers. Confederate Museum. Richmond.

Hunter McGuire Papers. Tompkins-McCaw Library. Virginia Commonwealth University, Richmond.

Hunter McGuire Papers. Virginia State Historical Society. Richmond.

James Boswell Diary.

Jedediah Hotchkiss Papers. Library of Congress. Washington, D.C.

Pendleton Family Papers. Southern Historical Society Collection. Chapel Hill: University of North Carolina Library.

Pendleton Papers. Southern Historical Society Collection. Chapel Hill.

*Richmond Daily Enquirer.*

*Richmond Daily Dispatch.*

*Richmond Times Dispatch.*

Thomas J. Jackson Papers. Confederate Museum. Richmond.

Thomas J. Jackson Papers. Virginia Military Institute. Lexington.

William Allan Papers. Southern Historical Society Collection. Chapel Hill.

## SECONDARY SOURCES

Alvey, Edward, Jr. *The History of the Presbyterian Church of Fredericksburg, Virginia, 1808–1976.*

# Bibliography

Bean, W. G. *The Liberty Hall Volunteers.* Charlottesville, 1964.

———. *Stonewall Jackson's Man: Sandie Pendleton.* Chapel Hill, 1959.

Blackford, Charles. *Letters from Lee's Army.* New York, 1947.

Bushong, Millard. *General Turner Ashby.* Staunton, 1980.

Cartmell, T. K. *History of Frederick County, Virginia.* Winchester, 1909.

Casler, John O. *Four Years in the Stonewall Brigade.* Girard, Kansas. 1893.

Chamberlain, Joshua. *Passing of the Armies.* New York, 1915.

Couper, William. *One Hundred Years at Virginia Military Institute.* Memorial Edition. Richmond, 1939.

Dabney, Robert L. *The Life and Campaigns of Lieut.-General Thomas J. Jackson.* New York, 1886.

Douglas, Henry Kyd. *I Rode with Stonewall.* Chapel Hill, 1940.

Divine, John, and others. *Loudoun County and the Civil War.* Leesburg, 1961.

Eisenschiml, Otto. "Medicine in the Civil War." *Civil War Times* (May 1962).

Evans, Clement A., ed. *Confederate Military History.* 13 vols. Atlanta, 1899.

Freeman, Douglas S. *Lee's Lieutenants.* New York, 1943.

Frye, Dennis. *The Second Virginia Infantry.* Lynchburg, 1984.

Gavin, James. *Toward Berlin.* New York, 1978.

Gerrish, Theodore, and John S. Hutchinson. *The Blue and the Gray.* Bangor, Maine, 1884.

Hamilton, J. G., ed. *The Papers of Randolph Shotwell.* Raleigh, 1929.

Happell, Ralph. *Last Days of Jackson.* Richmond, 1971.

Hassler, William. *A. P. Hill: Lee's Forgotten General.* Richmond, 1957.

Henderson, Colonel G. F. R. *Stonewall Jackson and the American Civil War.* New York, 1905.

Holland, J. W. *Jefferson Medical College of Philadelphia, Class of 1899 Yearbook.*

"Hunter McGuire, General Thomas J. Jackson." *Southern Historical Society Papers,* vol. 19. Richmond, 1891.

Hutchinson, Richard T. "Jonathan Letterman, 1824–1872." U.S. Army Medical Service, 1965.

Imboden, John G. "Jackson at Harpers Ferry in 1861." In *Battles and Leaders of the Civil War.* Vol. 2. New York, 1887.

Jackson, Mary Anna. *Memoirs of Stonewall Jackson.* Louisville, 1895.

*Journal of the American Medical Association* (September 29, 1900).

Keen, W. W. *Military Surgery in 1861–1865.* See footnote 36, p. 138.

Kinsolving, Roberta Corbin. "Stonewall Jackson in Winter Quarters: Memories of Moss Neck in the Winter of 1862." *Confederate Veteran,* vol. 20.

Lee, Susan P., ed. *The Memoirs of William Nelson Pendleton.* Philadelphia, 1893.

# Bibliography

McDonald, Archie P., ed. "Make Me a Map of the Valley." *Civil War Journal of Jackson's Topographer.* Dallas, 1973.

McDonald, Cornelia Peake. *A Diary with Reminiscences of the War and Refugee Life in the Shenandoah Valley, 1860–1865.* Nashville, 1934.

McGuire, Hunter H. Inaugural Address to the American Medical Association. *Journal of the American Medical Association* (June 23, 1893).

McGuire, Hunter. "The Wounding and Death of Stonewall Jackson." *Richmond Medical Journal* (May 1866).

McGuire, Hunter Holmes, and George L. Christian. *The Confederate Cause and Conduct in the War Between the States.* Richmond, 1907.

Miller, Francis T. *The Photographic History of the Civil War.* New York, 1911.

Morton, Frederic. *The Story of Winchester in Virginia.* Strasburg, 1925.

Munford, Beverly M. *Virginia's Attitude Toward Slavery and Succession.* Richmond, 1909.

Nevins, Allan, ed. *A Diary of the Civil War, 1860–1865.* This is the diary of George Strong. New York, 1962.

Newton, E. D. *The Red Cross Society Its Origin and Its First Practical Adoption.* New Orleans, April 25, 1906.

Owen, William M. *A History of the Washington Artillery.* Boston, 1885.

Palfrey, Francis W. *The Antietam and Fredericksburg.* New York, 1882.

Poague, William T. *Gunner with Stonewall.* Jackson, Tenn., 1957.

Pond, George E. *The Shenandoah Valley in 1864.* New York, 1883.

Quaife, Milo, ed. *Alphesus S. Williams: Letters from the Cannon's Mouth.* Detroit, 1959.

Quarles, Garland R. *The Streets of Winchester.* Winchester, 1958.

Ritter, Ben. "Jackson's First War-time Portrait, the Widow's Favorite." *Civil War Illustrated* (February 1979).

Robertson, James I. *The Stonewall Brigade.* Baton Rouge, 1959.

Lee Roirdan. "Battlefield Medicine." Jefferson Medical School Library.

Sheridan, Philip. *Personal Memoirs of Philip H. Sheridan.* New York, 1888.

Smith, James P. "With Stonewall Jackson." *Southern Historical Society Papers,* vol. 5. Richmond, 1920.

Stanard, William G. *The McGuire Family in Virginia.* Richmond, 1926.

Sullivan, James W. *Boyhood Memories of the Civil War, 1861–1865.* Carlisle, 1933.

Tanner, Robert G. *Stonewall in the Valley.* New York, 1976.

Taylor, Richard H. *Destruction and Reconstruction.* New York, 1879.

Trowbridge, John T. *The Desolate South.* New York, 1906.

U.S. Army Medical Service. *200 Years of Military Medicine.* Frederick, Md., 1975.

U.S. War Department, comp. *War of the Rebellion: A Compilation of the Official Records of the Union and Confederate Armies.* Washington, D.C., 1880–1891.

U.S. War Department, comp. *War of the Rebellion: The Medical and Surgical History of the War of the Rebellion.* Washington, D.C., 1875–1888.

Vandiver, Frank. *Mighty Stonewall.* New York, 1957.

Von Borcke, Heros. *Memoirs of the Confederate War for Independence.* Vol. 1. New York, 1931.

Wagner, Frederick B. "The Making of a Medical School." *Jefferson Medical School Alumni Bulletin* (winter 1980).

Weaver, George H. *Bulletin of the Society of Medical History of Chicago* (January 1933).

Wiley, Bell I. *The Life of Johnny Reb.* New York, 1971.

———. *They Who Fought Here.* New York, 1959.

Worsham, John. *One of Jackson's Four Cavalry.* New York, 1912.

Worthington, Glenn H. *Fighting for Time.* Frederick, Md., 1933.

# Index

**A**

American Medical Association, 114–16, 129
Antietam Creek, 61, 62, 63
Appomattox Court House, Va., 110
Army of the Shenandoah, 10, 14, 28

**B**

Banks, Nathaniel, 32, 38, 40, 41
Berkeley Springs, W.Va., 30, 34
Berryville, Va., 2, 65
Boswell, James, 54, 73, 74, 93
Bower, The, 66
Bowling Green, Va., 93
Breckinridge, John C., 6, 96–98
Bristoe Station, Va., 91
Brown, John, 4
Bunker Hill, W.Va., 10, 65–67, 73

**C**

Carlisle, Pa., 88–89
Caroline County, Va., 93
Cashtown, Pa., 89, 96
Cedar Creek, Va., 103
Centreville, Va., 30
Chancellorsville, Va., 76, 85
Chantilly, Va., 57
Chesapeake & Ohio Canal, 31
Conrad's Store, Va., 36–38
Corbin, Jane, 72, 74
Corbin, Katherine (Kate), 71, 72, 73, 75, 92, 93
Corbin, Richard, 71, 72
Corbin, Roberta, 71, 93
Cracker Barrel Conference, 76
Cross Keys, Va., 41

Culpeper, Va., 86
Cussons, John, 121

**D**

Dabb House, Va., 54
Dabney, Robert L., 15, 91
Davis, Jefferson, 17, 36, 84
Douglas, Henry K., 10, 32, 54, 61, 65–66, 71–72, 84–85, 87–88, 89–94, 96, 105, 107, 123

**E**

Early, Jubal A., 96–100, 102, 106
Epidemics, 21–22
Ewell, Richard S., 36–37, 56–57, 86, 87, 88, 89, 91

**F**

Falling Waters, Va., 14
Fisher's Hill, Va., 100, 101
Frederick, Md., 59–61, 69, 70, 88, 97–98
Fredericksburg, Va., 69, 72, 73, 74
Frémont, John, 40
Front Royal, Va., 37

**G**

Gallaher, Dewitt Clinton, 105–6
Gallaher, Sally, 105, 106, 109
Garnett, Richard, 34
Gettysburg, Pa., 89–91
Gordonsville, Va., 54
Graham, James, 29, 31, 32
Grant, Ulysses S., 94, 96, 99
Gregg, Maxcy, 70
Guiney's or Guinea Station, Va., 80–84

# Index

## H

Hagerstown, Md., 96
Hamilton's Crossing, Va., 74, 75
Harman, John, 32, 59
Harpers Ferry, Va., 4, 7, 8, 9, 10, 60, 61, 62
Harrisburg, Pa., 88
Henderson, G. F. R., 118–21
Hill, Ambrose P., 57, 61, 62, 72, 89
Hoge, Moses, 55, 117–18, 126
Hotchkiss, Jedediah, 35, 36, 58–59, 70–71, 73, 119–20, 123–24
Hunter, David, 96

## I

Imboden, John, 89–90

## J

Jackson, Mary Ann, 29, 32, 55, 75, 82, 84
Jackson, Thomas, 2
  at VMI, 8
  ordered to Harpers Ferry, 8
  train troops, 9
  at Falling Waters, Va., 14
  at Paris, Va., 15
  at First Manassas, 16–17
  Romney campaign, 31
  Braddock Street, 31
  Winchester, 32–33
  Valley campaign, 34–41
  Sharpsburg, 61, 62
  button, sewn by, 66
  Fredericksburg, 68
  Moss Neck, 71–72
  wounding of, 76–77
  death of, 83
  burial of, 84–85

## K

Kenly, John, 30, 37
Kernstown, Va., 34, 40, 89

## L

Leesburg, Va., 58
Letcher, John, 6–7
Letterman, Jonathan, 13
Lexington, Va., 9, 40, 60, 67, 69, 85, 96, 100, 119, 120
Liberty Hall Volunteers, 9

## M

Massanutten Mountains, 37
McDonald, Cornelia, 6, 7, 66, 68, 87, 91, 105
McGuire, Ann Moss, 3, 108
McGuire, Edward, 1, 2
McGuire, Edward, Jr., 2
McGuire, Elizabeth Holmes, 2
McGuire, Hugh (brother), 3, 50, 105–7
McGuire, Hugh Holmes (father), 2, 3, 7, 67
McGuire, Hunter Holmes
  birth of, 3
  childhood of, 3
  education of, 3
  attends Jefferson Medical College, 4
  John Brown episode, 4
  at Tulane University, 4
  Harpers Ferry, 9
  brigade surgeon, 9
  description of First Manassas, 16, 17
  medical treatment to Jackson, 17
  returns to Winchester, 29
  medical treatment to R. S. Ewell, 56–57
  at Sharpsburg, 62
  at Fredericksburg, 70
  at Moss Neck, 72
  death of Janie Corbin, 74
  wounding of Jackson, 77
  Jackson's death, 84
  medical doctor of Second Corps, ANV, 94
  marital engagement, 93
  suffers stroke, 125
  death of, 125
McGuire, Mary Stuart, 93
Meade, George G., 88, 91
Medical School of Virginia, 2
Middletown, Md., 96
Milroy, Robert, 37, 87
Mitchell, Mary B., 63–64
Monocacy River, 97–98
Moore, Samuel Preston, 11–13
Morton Hall, Va., 91–92
Moss Neck Manor, Va., 71–75, 92–93
Mount Jackson, Va., 32

## N

Narrow Passage, Va., 35

## P

Palfrey, Francis, 62–63
Pendleton, Alexander Swift "Sandie," 14, 21, 32, 35, 54–55, 59, 65, 71–75, 84–85, 86–88, 92–93, 100–101
Pope, John, 55
Port Republic, Va., 40–41
Port Royal, Va., 70
Potomac River, 14, 32, 36, 58, 61, 96

## R

Ramseur, Stephen D., 96–98, 102, 103

# Index

ransom note, 96–97
Reagan, Ronald, 133
Robb, Charles, 133
Romney, W.Va., 31

## S

St. Luke's, 53
Second Manassas, 56–57
Sharpsburg, Md., 61, 63, 65
Shepherdstown, W.Va., 61–65, 96
Sheridan, Philip, 98, 101, 102–3, 106, 112
Shields, James, 21, 38
Smith, James P., 59–60, 71, 75, 76, 77, 78, 79, 88, 123
South Mountain, Md., 60–61, 96
Spotsylvania, Va., 95
Staunton, Va., 93, 107, 110, 111

## T

Taylor, Richard, 36

## U

United Confederate Veterans, 121

## W

Wallace, Lew, 97
Washington, George, 1
Waynesboro, Va., 105
Wheeler, Susannah, 2
White's Ford, 58
White, William, 85, 100
Wilderness, 94
Willis, Edward, 95
Winchester, Va., 1, 2, 3, 4, 6, 7, 15, 29, 31, 32, 33, 34, 35, 39, 40, 67, 68, 86, 88, 98, 104, 119
Wolseley, Garnet, 67, 118, 119, 126
Wood, Joseph, 1

## Y

Yerby, Thomas, 74–75